S0-ADH-961

DATE DUE

The St. Nicholas Series
EDITED BY THE REV. DOM BEDE CAMM, O.S.B.

THE ANGELICAL
CARDINAL

REGINALD POLE

Nibil Obstat.

D. BEDA CAMM
Censor Deputatus

Imprimatur:

✠ GULIELMUS *Episcopus Arindelensis*
Vicarius Generalis

WESTMONASTERII,
die 14 *Januarii*, 1908

The St. Nicholas Series

EDITED BY THE REV. DOM BEDE CAMM, O.S.B.

LIST OF VOLUMES

Each Volume is in Foolscap 8vo, and has Six Illustrations reproduced by the three-colour process.
Price 2s. per volume.

Cardinal Pole.

THE ANGELICAL CARDINAL

REGINALD POLE

Non Anglus, sed Angelus vocetur

BY

C. M. ANTONY

WITH A PREFACE BY

FATHER ROBERT HUGH BENSON

LONDON
MACDONALD AND EVANS
4 ADAM STREET, ADELPHI
1909

Printed by BALLANTYNE & Co. LIMITED
Tavistock Street, Covent Garden, London

TO

THE VERY REV.

FATHER REGINALD BUCKLER

O.P.

PREFATORY NOTE

THE history of Cardinal Pole is the history of the great schism and great reconciliation of England. The two are so intimately bound up in each other that it is impossible to write of one without the other; and this must be the author's apology for her frequent reference to contemporary history.

Over the shadowy, bloodstained stage pass stately historic figures of Pope and Emperor, King and Cardinal, Saint and Martyr, Nun and Queen; great statesmen and powerful prelates; while the background is alive with crowding faces—monk, friar, ambassador, assassin, student, servant, friend and traitor, each with his part to play in the stately drama of that tragedy called the Life of Reginald Pole.

It has been the writer's endeavour to seek to outline, as far as possible, the personality and character of " the Angelical Cardinal,"

PREFATORY NOTE

by means of contemporary records and letters, quoted in or translated from the original, rather than in her own words. Her most grateful thanks are due, for valuable help given in several ways, to her friends, the Very Rev. Fr. Reginald Buckler O.P.; Father Robert Hugh Benson; and three Fathers of the Solêsmes Benedictine Monastery at Farnborough, whose kindness and sympathy has been unbounded.

Also to another priest, through whose generosity she was able to undertake this book, which, but for him, would never have been written.

C. M. ANTONY.

WOODCHESTER.
Feast of the Epiphany, 1909.

PREFACE

IT is hardly possible to imagine a character less suited, in popular estimation to the needs of his time, than was that of Reginald Pole to the period of the English schism. They were days of fierceness, brutality and literally Machiavellian diplomacy; and the nature of the Cardinal who played so great a part in them was one of gentleness, kindness and simple transparence. It was an age when scholars suffered for their knowledge of the truth, Christians for their fidelity, and citizens of God's Kingdom for that loyalty that includes, but transcends also, patriotism: from a merely temporal point of view it was almost an advantage to be ignorant, unconscientious and selfish.

It is no wonder then that the Cardinal, a lover of peace and study, sensitive in conscience and passionately zealous for souls, should, as the world reckons success, have failed in nearly every task to which he set his hand. He failed in his first legation to England, and in his second legation to the continental sovereigns ; and his success in the reconciliation of his country to the Holy See was, as he foresaw perfectly well, no more than temporary. Finally he failed before men to keep even that reputation for which alone he cared, that is, his reputation as a perfect Catholic Christian, and died under the suspicion of heresy.

Yet, as history gradually justifies the ways of God to men, every increase of our knowledge of the past goes steadily, though unsensationally, to lift Pole's failure up to that victory which is alone really worth the winning. While kings betrayed their trust, and even popes did not whole-heartedly maintain it—while Henry VIII. lost his soul and Paul IV. his head—Reginald Pole at least retained his Christian innocence and counted all things but loss if he might win Christ. He prayed, he adventured himself, he went to and fro in simpleness of intention and utter self-sacrifice ; his mother died tragically in the cause for which he laboured, and himself had to bear the reproach that he would have done better if he had died himself in the same manner. Yet, if the actual affairs in which he was employed came to unhappy issues, the fault was never in their agent, neither as regarded his capacities nor his goodwill. Failure to perform an impossible task has, more than once in history, been the occasion of a startling personal success.

As regards the suspicion of heresy under which he fell, it is unnecessary to say even a word in refutation. For his nature was the precise counterpart of that of which self-choosers are made. At Bethlehem there came to the cradle of God two classes of persons, the wise and the simple, the kings and the shepherds ; it was the *bourgeois* who remained at home. The significance is to be found in every age of religious unrest. And it was Cardinal Pole, above all others, who combined in himself the characteristic of king and shepherd. His learning was profound, and his simplicity equally profound. So he, with More and Fisher, and a hundred more, retained the Faith, while Henry, Cranmer, and Cromwell lost it. . . .

As regards his attitude towards the penalties inflicted in the name of religion during Henry's reign in England, it is necessary to

say a word or two, although, as a brilliant
writer has recently remarked, it is a hopeless
task, in this age of sentimentality and
extravagant humanitarianism—among persons who fear death more than sin and
regard pain as the greatest of evils—to
discuss the matter with the hope of a fair
hearing. First, however, it must be remembered that the Protestantism of that date
was of a totally different character, morally
as well as dogmatically, from that into
which it has since developed. Now it
stands, on the moral side for a harmless
individualism, often coupled with a real
personal piety, alike granting and demanding
toleration—an individualism, which, from
the very fact of its denial of a Living Authority
in matters of Faith can indeed imagine no
higher virtue than toleration and which in
matters of State at any rate, is essentially
indifferentist. But in Tudor days it stood
rather for anarchy and even coercion ; and
Henry and Elizabeth—Nationalists rather
than strict Protestants—recognised this no
less than Mary. Denying authority in
religion it denied that which stood behind
all the European governments of that date
and its significance is brought out unmistak-

ably by the fact that all the seditious movements against Mary were inaugurated and wrought in its name. To deny then authority in matters of faith was to raise the presumption of anarchy and to merit the penalties inflicted by the State, in self-defence, upon all who menaced its claim upon obedience;—for it was the Commons of England, and not primarily ecclesiastics nor the Queen herself who demanded these penalties.

Pole's attitude then was one of simple acquiescence in the methods of the time, as might be the acquiescence of a tender-hearted chaplain who stands behind the judge when sentence of death is given. If he did not raise his voice against the principle of punishment, at least he did not raise it upon the other side. It is ludicrous to compare him even for an instant to such a man as Henry himself who hanged the Carthusians for asserting the Pope's supremacy and burned Frith for impugning the sacrament of the altar. While Bonner and Gardiner are accused of rigidity and even truculence, no such accusation was made against Pole. It was, indeed, his leniency on a certain occasion towards some followers of Luther

PREFACE

that brought his orthodoxy under suspicion. And this is the more remarkable, when we reflect upon the manner in which he himself had suffered under parallel circumstances.

It is to be hoped then that this volume will not only bring the name of Reginald Pole back into remembrance, but will also detach the truth, as illustrated in his life and adventures, from the all but inextricable tangle of falsehood, deliberate and unintended, with which it has been confused in the minds of English readers.

ROBERT HUGH BENSON.

SAN SILVESTRO, ROME,
March, 1909.

CONTENTS

LIST OF ILLUSTRATIONS

xvii

CATALOGUE OF THE PRINCIPAL WORKS WRITTEN BY CARDINAL POLE

(Compiled from Catalogues in British Museum.)

1. R.P. . . . ad Henricū Octavū Brittaniæ Regem pro Ecclesiasticæ Unitatis defensione. Libri quatuor. Fol. Romæ. (1535–6). (Later editions, 1555 Strasbourg, and 1587.)

2. De Pace (treatise on peace between Charles V. and Henry II.) *Circa* 1555–6. Romæ.

3. De Concilio Liber. De Baptismo Constanti Magni. (Dedicated to Paul IV.) Romæ. 1562.

4. De Summo Pontifice Christi in terris vicario. Lovanii. 1569.

5. Copia d'una Lettera d'Angleterra nella quale narra l'entrata del Card : Polo in Inghilterra per la conversione di quella Isola alla Fede Catholica. Milano, 1554.

6. Copia delle Lettere del Rè d'Inghilterra è del Card. Polo sopra la reduzione di quel Regno alla unione della Chiesa. (Date uncertain.) *Circa* 1557.

7. Reformatio Angliæ ex decretis R.P. Sedis Apostolicæ Legati, anno 1556. Quarto. Romæ. 1562.

CATALOGUE OF PRINCIPAL WORKS

8. Apologia R.P. ad Carolum V. Cæsarem (being the dedication to the Emperor prefixed to a copy of " De Unitate ").

9. Unitatis Ecclesiæ defensio ad Edwardum, Henrici filium. (Lovanii. 1569.)

10. A treatise of Justification, found among the writings of Cardinal Pole. (Lovanii, 1569.)

11. Longolii vita. (His first published work.) Padua (?) 1524.

12. Epistolarum R.P. . . . et aliorum et ipsum. Edited by Cardinal Quirini. Brixiæ. 1744.

PEDIGREE OF CARDINAL POLE

(Abridged from that in the Heralds' office.)

Edward III., 1327–1377.

Edmund Langley, D. of York (5th son)

Richard, E. of Cambridge (2nd son).

Richard, D. of York, and E. of Cambridge. Killed at Wakefield, 1460.

George, D. of Clarence, E. of Warwick and Salisbury.

Margaret Plantagenet = Sir Richard Pole.
(Countess of Salisbury)

Arthur Pole.   Geoffrey Pole, d. 1557.   REGINALD POLE, 1500–1558.   Ursula Pole. Lady Stafford.

Edward IV., 1461 (D. of York).

Henry VII. = Elizabeth.
(Tudor.)
(1485)

Henry, Lord Montague, d. 1538.

Henry VIII. (1509).

Mary 1553.   Elizabeth. 1558.   Edward VI. 1547.

xxi

CHAPTER I

BIRTH, EDUCATION, AND EARLY LIFE,
1500–1526

REGINALD POLE, the fourth and youngest son of Sir Richard Pole, and his wife Margaret Countess of Salisbury, was born on March 3, 1500, at Stourton Castle, Staffordshire.

His father, the representative of an ancient and honourable Welsh family, was in high favour at the Court of Henry VII., under whom he had served in Scotland ; and the king had appointed him, on account of his valour and accomplishments, to be chief gentleman-of-the-bedchamber to his elder son, Arthur, Prince of Wales. He died a few years after Reginald's birth.

Through his mother, Blessed Margaret Pole, daughter of George Duke of Clarence, niece of Edward IV., and only sister and heiress of that unfortunate Earl of Warwick long in prison on a charge of pretended treason, and finally beheaded by Henry VII.,

Reginald was of purely royal descent. In his veins ran the blood of the ancient houses of England, Spain, France, and Castile ; but an even greater distinction was to be his. He was destined to be the son of a martyr, " which," as he wrote in 1541, " is certainly grander than to be born of any royal house." *

Of his three brothers, the eldest, Henry Lord Montague, was beheaded in 1539 on Tower Hill, nominally for high treason ; in reality for sympathy with his exiled brother and for opposing Henry VIII.'s supremacy. The second, Geoffrey, seems to have been a rather restless person, much mixed up in political schemes. It was his evidence, extorted under fear of torture and death, which was instrumental in the condemnation of his mother and elder brother, and for which the grateful Henry granted him a free pardon. The third brother, Arthur, was sentenced to death under Elizabeth, but reprieved, on account of his relationship to the Queen. His only sister, Ursula, married Lord Stafford, son of the Duke of Buckingham.

Reginald Pole's mother, as we learn from

* " Venetian Calendar." Vol. v. 108.

their letters to each other, offered him unreservedly, at his birth, to God ; and so
perfect was her trust that she took no pains
to provide for his education and future,
willing that her son should owe even his
temporal welfare directly to God, and not
to her. Nor was she disappointed of her
hope, for Henry VIII., Reginald's second
cousin, before his succession in 1509, under-
took the entire charge of the little boy's
education, and when he was only seven,
sent him to school as mediæval custom
was—to the Carthusians at Sheen, where he
spent five happy years, and developed
unusual intellectual gifts. His parents seem
to have always intended him for the priesthood ; and his character and peculiar gifts
all tended to an ecclesiastical career.

When he was twelve he went to Oxford
and entered at Magdalen, where he was called
a " nobleman of the college," and had an
apartment in the president's house. Henceforward we find such entries as these in
the King's Book of Payments : " To
Reginald Pole . . . for his exhibition at
school this year, £12." * This was on
March 28, 1512, and on June 8 of the next

* " Letters and Papers of Henry VIII." Vol. ii. p. 2.

year there is another: " For Reginald Pole, student in the University of Oxford, Pension which the . . . Prior of St. Frideswide is bound to give to a clerk of the King's nomination, until he be promoted to a competent benefice by the said Prior." *

At Oxford he made extraordinary progress. The great Renaissance movement, then spreading all over Europe, had reached the English universities. Students and scholars everywhere were learning to love learning for its own sake, and to read the wealth of classic literature in the languages in which it was written. England, however, was behind the Continent. Though Oxford could boast of Linacre and Latimer, men whose names were of European fame, the study of Greek in the universities was neglected, chiefly from a lack of capable teachers.* Notwithstanding, Linacre, the King's physician, a sound scholar, and man of ready wit, may, with his friend Latimer, lay claim to have been the true restorer of learning in England, and to have laid the foundation of that reputation which Oxford now enjoys.

Under these masters Reginald Pole pro-

* " Letters and Papers of Henry VIII." Vol. ii.

gressed as fast as even they could desire. He could " dispute for thirty days in logic and ethics," had a ripe knowledge of Latin, and a graceful knack of writing clever Latin verse. The thought of the priesthood seems to have been, for the present, put aside to allow more time for the fascinating study of " polite learning "—always a passion with Pole.

His friendship with Blessed Thomas More seems to have begun at Oxford, in connection with which a charming little story comes down to us. The future Lord Chancellor was ill, and sent to Oxford for medical advice. Pole happened to hear of this, and hastened to collect the very highest opinions upon More's case which the university could afford. Linacre, no doubt, was consulted ; and the prescription thus obtained was sent home by Pole to his mother, the Countess of Salisbury, to be made up for the invalid. Long after this More speaks of the great pleasure caused him by Pole's commendation of a Latin letter written by his favourite daughter, Margaret. The friendship was life-long, though the friends saw but little of each other.

In 1515 Pole took his B.A. degree, for

which we read that he petitioned to have " a gown and robes suitable ; " and also for admission to the public library. As was customary with intending candidates for the priesthood, especially those of noble family, Pole was presented by Henry VIII. with the titles and revenues of several benefices, though he was not yet even in minor orders ; but he was responsible for the maintenance of priests, at his own charges, to fulfil the duties which he was incapable of undertaking himself. In Pole's case this obligation was rigidly carried out. In 1517 he became Prebendary of Roscombe, " in the Cathedral Church of Salisbury," and of Yatminster, or Gatcombe Secunda, in the same diocese. On February 12, 1518, " Reginald Poole, clk," was presented to the " collegiate church of Wynbourne Mynstre, Salisbury diocese ; " * and about the same time he received the appointment of Dean of Exeter.

But he had no intention of settling down quietly to enjoy these preferments. For some years he had felt the need of a more perfect study of Greek. Much as he loved Oxford, much as he owed to it, it was only

* "Letters and Papers of Henry VIII." Vol. ii. p. 2.

on the Continent that his desire could be fulfilled. His eyes turned, not to the brilliant university of Paris, but to Italy—to the wonderful city in which at that time the greatest scholars in the world, with perhaps one exception, were gathered. His mother, who loved him intensely, understood his longing and gave her consent. His tutors at Oxford approved. The king promised him an allowance of 500 crowns yearly, beyond his ecclesiastical revenues of 1000 crowns ; and in February 1521 we find the first entry of this in the King's Book of Payments : " to Mr. Pole, whom the King sends to Italy, finding for one year, £100." And so, at the close of 1520, Reginald Pole, crowned with university honours, left Oxford for Padua.

On April 1, 1521, King Henry sent a message to the Signory of Venice, recommending "a nephew" of his, "the Lord Reginald . . . who is going to study at Padua ; " * and on May 21 of the same year a patent was made out for " Sir Reginald Pole, a kinsman of the King of England, who is come to study at Padua," authorising him to export plate, clothes, &c.†

* " Venetian Calendar." Vol. v. 184.   † *Ibid.* 218.

THE ANGELICAL CARDINAL

The ancient city of Padua, in the fifteenth and sixteenth centuries was in truth the Athens of Europe. Annexed by Venice, after a long and chequered history, in the year 1406, the city of St. Antony had become the centre to which all the greatest scholars, thinkers, and *literati* of the day were instinctively attracted. Its noble university was the pride of Italy and the world. The humanities, physics, logic, rhetoric, ethics, science, here found their most subtle exponents and professors. No branch of literature, ancient or modern, was neglected, but the study of Greek was considered of paramount importance, and took precedence of that of any other language. Pope Leo X., himself a brilliant man of letters, was a patron of the University of Padua, and in Pole's day to have studied there was the highest distinction obtainable by any scholar.

The city, with its picturesque, cobbled, arcaded streets, its many-arched bridges, and massive walls and towers, has probably changed but little since the days when the young English student, enthusiastic and sensitively receptive, rode with his well-appointed retinue through the fertile country of northern Italy, where Antony the Miracle Worker, dead for 300 years, lived as "the Saint," in the hearts of the people just as he lives, a vivid reality, to-day.

It must have been a journey quick with strange new impressions. After the gigantic barrier of snow-capped Alps behind them had faded into the clouds, and the beautiful mountain-country, richly wooded, or grey and barren, furrowed with the stony beds of rapid-rushing rivers had been left behind, the road ran for many miles across a richly cultivated plain which a few months later would be thick with leafy vineyards and miles of flower-meadows and corn-fields ; and which even then in early spring must have been a fragrant sea of flowering orchards, rosy apple-blossom and snowy pear ; and leagues of pale pink peach-bloom beyond the cold brown fields—a feast of colour.

It was the country that he loved, and to which his thoughts, until his death, continually turned. Here and there would be a little brown red-roofed town, clustering round some ancient hoary castle, whose turrets were visible far across the plain ; and everywhere, like the masts of distant ships rose the slender shafts of the village *campanili*.

And then at last the grey walls of the city, with its fortress-like Duomo, and two vast Basilicas ; in whose picturesque streets and market-place gaily dressed peasants met and mingled with students and scholars from England and France, Germany and Spain, Greece and the Low Countries—men of all ranks and of almost every nation under heaven.

No wonder Pole, from the beginning, felt at home there. He carried introductions to the heads of the university, and his arrival seems to have created a certain sensation in Padua which was in nowise lessened during his six years' residence there. He took a suitable house and, as was customary amongst wealthy students, especially those of noble blood, he set about forming a " household " of learned men, by whose conversation and companionship he could profit daily, and whose instruction would be most valuable in his studies. The chief of these was Longolius, a young and brilliant Fleming, one of the most gifted men in the university, a genius who made his mark on his age, though he died

when only thirty-four, before the great
work of his life was finished ; his dying message, in a touching letter, being to Reginald
Pole, to whom he left his library. He had
undertaken to refute the heresy of the
apostate Luther, but only one of the five
great volumes of the treatise was completed
before his early death. He had an absolute
mastery of the Latin tongue, which even
in the days when it was the common language
of the learned, marked him out as the most
brilliant orator and faultless writer of
Latin prose and verse in the university.
Under another great professor, Leonicus,
Reginald Pole studied his beloved Greek ;
and a third member of the household was
Thomas Lupset, the young secretary of
the English Ambassador at Venice, with
whom Pole formed a warm friendship.
Here, too, were Thomas Starkey, who
became a few years later so conspicuous
a feature in Pole's life ; John Bonamico ; and a young Venetian noble, Count
Bembo, perhaps Pole's greatest friend in
Padua.

For his character and personality were
unusually attractive ; all Padua considered
him as a member of the English royal

family * and was correspondingly proud of him. He was young, rich, gifted ; possessed great charm of manner, and an eager and ingenuous enthusiasm which seems to have won all hearts. His great natural modesty, and a certain simplicity and directness, together with a gravity in some respects beyond his years balanced his more brilliant qualities and gave his judgment a weight which was respected not only in the university, but a few years later by Henry VIII. himself, on the question which was to convulse Christendom. With Aloysius Priuli, another representative of a noble Venetian house, Pole formed a friendship which lasted until his death ; and for which Priuli gladly sacrificed his prospects and destined career, forsaking everything to become the companion and secretary of the man who was dearest to him on earth.

The famous Erasmus, the greatest scholar in Europe, was then at Padua, and was greatly attracted by the young Englishman. In his letters at this time there are several references to Pole, dwelling not only on his

* Bembo calls him, in a letter; "Il Monsignor d'Inghilterra, il più propinquo che habbia quel Rè."

brilliant attainments, but his personal charm and character. He seems to have impressed every one who knew him.

On March 26, 1523, we find an entry in the annals of the Council of Ten to enjoin their " Governors of Padua . . . to permit the Most Illustrious and Reverend Reginald Pole, British-born, a student in our University to carry weapons there . . . he and four of his servants, for the security of his person . . . according to his request made through the English Ambassador." * This ambassador was an old friend, Dr. Richard Pace, of whom we hear more two years later, when on February 6, 1525, *en route* for Venice he visited " the King's nephew " at Padua ; and it was with him that Pole stayed when he visited Venice the following June. " It is Corpus Christi Day, and the Doge, clad in cloth of gold, with a crimson satin mantle and crimson ducal cap, came to Mass in St. Mark's Church, with the ambassadors from the Pope, England, Austria, Milan, Ferrara and Mantua. . . . Behind them, with the councillors, was the nephew of the King of England, who is studying at Padua, and who walked with . . . [the]

* " Letters and Papers of Henry VIII." Vol. v. p. 12.

Bishop of Paphos," * A year later, in July 1526, after his visit to Rome, we find him at Venice again, on the occasion of the magnificent pageants organised at the publication of the Holy League. " The only personage in the [Doge's ?] palace was the cousin of the King of England, by name Reginald Pole. He is studying at Padua, and came hither to the house of the English ambassador to see this pageant which was a very beautiful one." † In September of the same year he was still at Padua, for : " the English ambassador has gone to Padua [from Venice] to visit the relation of the King who is studying there." ‡

In 1524 Dr. Fox made him a Fellow of the new college of Corpus Christi at Oxford, of which he was the founder ; and this distinction gave at least as much pleasure to his Italian friends as to Pole himself.

In 1525 he paid a short visit to Rome, setting out with a small retinue, and intending to travel very quietly, as became a pilgrim to the Holy City. But to his surprise he found himself *fêted* and honoured wherever he went. When he arrived at

---

* "Venetian Calendar." Vol. iii. 1042.
† *Ibid.* 1343. ‡ *Ibid.* 1405.

Verona Monsignor Ghiberti, the bishop, a personal stranger to him, came out and welcomed him with great courtesy and affection, and Pole discovered that it was to this prelate that he owed the reception with which he had met at every halting-place on his journey. He was deeply touched by Ghiberti's kindness, and the bishop became one of his closest friends; one indeed to whom he turned at all times for sympathy and encouragement.

His stay in Rome was short. After visiting the Holy Places he returned to Padua by way of Verona without being presented at the Papal Court, probably for political reasons. At the close of 1526 he returned, by the king's wish, to England; and at his command, to Court.

His public career was now to begin. Henceforth Reginald Pole was to help to make English history.

CHAPTER II

ON what was probably the first occasion on which Henry VIII. saw Reginald Pole after his return from Italy he told him openly that in all his travels he could not have met the equal of Blessed John Fisher, Bishop of Rochester, for virtue and learning—a statement which shows that at that time this prelate had not lost all his influence over his former pupil, and that Henry was not yet dead to all honour and gratitude.

But the Court of England was becoming rapidly demoralised. The king's private life was a constant source of scandal to all and of bitter grief to the queen. At the moment of Pole's return Henry's fickle affections were violently engaged by Anne Bullen, a young lady-in-waiting to Queen Katherine ; of great personal beauty ; whose selfishness was only equalled by her ambition. She had no intention of becoming the laughing-stock of the Court, and Henry had been given to understand plainly that unless she became his wife she could have nothing to say to him. Finding it impossible to move her from this position, the king, while retaining her in great state in his wife's retinue, and taking advantage of every opportunity to be in her company, set his mind to that task which was to end in the upheaval of the Catholic Church in England.

In such an atmosphere Pole found it impossible to breathe. Making his excuses with some difficulty to his royal cousin he withdrew, under plea of continuing his studies, to Sheen, the home of his happy childhood. Here, within the enclosure, Dean Colet had built a handsome house, intending to end his days among his Carthusian friends. He died, however, almost before it was finished, and the house as it stood was now granted to Pole by Henry, and here for nearly two years he lived in great tranquillity and peace, continuing his studies, and leading a semi-monastic life. It was the calm before the storm—the storm which, outside the cloister, was beginning to blacken the whole horizon, causing men's hearts to fail and their minds to reel at the mere prospect of the yet inconceivable terror of it. And even now, as the sky grew steadily darker, the first drops fell.

Henry's conduct during the latter part of his reign is, perhaps, the most wonderful of all instances in history of a man of ungoverned will—which has become ungovernable—overriding heart, conscience, judgment, decency, laws both divine and human, and at the same time deluding himself with the idea (at any rate up to a certain point) that he is doing perfectly right and acting according to his conscience and the will of Almighty God. His whole career was in fact a sort of apotheosis of the Nonconformist Conscience.

But at first that difficult conscience, which took some time to kill, led him to seek sympathy—and, if possible, justification for his actions—from the men whose opinions he respected.

Unfortunately for Pole, he was one of these. The king did not in the least want the advice he asked for, and only desired people to agree with what he had already determined. He had by now decided to divorce the queen, whose husband he had been for twenty years; and as even Henry could find no excuse for such a deed in the blameless life of that unfortunate lady it occurred to him that perhaps valid objection might be taken to the fact that he had, under dispensation, married his brother Arthur's wife.

That Katherine had been only nominally, not actually married to his brother (who was in a very precarious state of health at the time); that Henry's union with her had been blessed by Pope Julius II.; that for the greater part of their long wedded life—during which several children had been born to them, of whom the Princess Mary alone survived)—they had lived on most affectionate terms; all these things were resolutely set aside by Henry, whose conscience now began to afflict him sadly; moved thereto, as he publicly announced, by his dread of having contracted an illegal marriage; but in reality, as the whole Court was now perfectly aware, by his insane passion for Anne Bullen. In 1527 Henry applied definitely to Pope Clement VII. for a divorce, to enable him to marry again, on the ground that there was no heir-male to the crown of England. In 1528, with almost inconceivable assurance he sent four agents to Rome to beg that either (1) Queen Katherine should be compelled to enter religion ; (2) that if she would not agree to this unless Henry did the like that he might be secretly dispensed beforehand, so that the queen being finally disposed of, he might leave his monastery, and marry : or, (3) if both these plans were negatived that he might have two wives, and that the Pope would legitimise the children of both marriages. Precedents for these proceedings —especially the last—were quoted from the book of Leviticus, and the messengers were instructed, if the Pope refused, to threaten that both his election and authority might be called in question. Clement VII., a weak but witty pontiff, retorted that no doubt Henry was fully acquainted with the tenets of the faith of which he professed himself the defender, and that if heresy arose, the king, not he, was responsible.

About this time, Reginald Pole, whose opinion on these matters had been unsuccessfully sought by the king, both directly and indirectly, met "at the Cardinal of York's palace," the man in whose hands

lay the destinies of England, Thomas
Cromwell, at that time in Wolsey's service.
Very cautiously and cleverly did that
astute statesman seek to fathom the mind
of the young student, but Pole was quite a
match for him, and has left us a delightful
account of the interview. Cromwell asked
him his opinion of a political work by an
Italian writer, and finding Pole had not read
it, "fell into a discourse on the necessary
qualifications of those who are called to the
councils of princes." Pole saw at once that
he was to be sifted on the question of the
divorce. "My answer was that I thought
it the duty of every such person, above all
other considerations, to advise what was
most conducive to his prince's honour and
interest, and enlarged myself, from the
dictates of reason and the best authors, on
the nature of Virtue, in which both Honour
and Interest are grounded."

Cromwell, quite unmoved by these considerations replied that these notions were
"very plausible when delivered in the Schools
or from the Pulpit, but were of little use in
the Cabinets of Kings, and, if much insisted
on, would create Hatred and Aversion to
the Adviser, as they seldom fall in with the

Prince's inclinations, and are quite foreign to what is practised in courts." Prudence and experience, continued the future Vice-gerent, were the qualities that really mattered, for without them " many promising states-men had forfeited their prince's favour and become useless "—a delicate but necessary euphuism—or had ruined themselves and their families.

The ingenuous speaker then gave several examples to prove his assertion, and con-cluded : " that the chief concern of a person in this station should be to study his prince's inclinations, in which much sagacity was required, as they sometimes lie disguised under appearances of a very different import : that it became kings to use the specious names of religion, equity, and other virtues, though their designs were not always regulated by them : that true ability lay in discovering what their real intentions were ; and then, in managing in such sort that they may attain their ends, and yet no open failure in religion or probity be observed : and that this ability was seen in proportion as the minister could reconcile the appearances of virtue, which princes were unwilling to give up, with the sub-

stantial interests of the State. That this
was a compendious way to secure favour
and authority with them, and to be useful
to oneself and others."

Thus the principal adviser of Henry VIII.,
of whom his auditor remarks that "if he
really thought as he spoke" and had been
Nero's counsellor when that monarch was
anxious to murder his mother, Cromwell
would have been "at no loss to justify the
parricide." Pole, however, "made no reply
to this barefaced impiety," though Cromwell, in repeating the conversation to the
king, put his own construction upon the
young man's silence. The views which he
had expressed, he told Pole, were most ably
set forth in the work to which he had
already alluded, and he begged to be allowed
to lend him the book. Pole refused diplo-
matically, but borrowed it from a friend,
and studied it carefully, unknown to Cromwell, coming to the conclusion that : " it
is such a performance that if Satan himself
were to leave a successor I do not well see
by what other maxims he would direct him
to reign ! "—an opinion certainly justified
by subsequent events.*

* "Life of Cardinal Pole." T. Phillips. Vol. i. 42–44.

The book upon which this judgment was passed was no other than *Il Principe*, by one Niccolo Machiavelli.

In 1528 the terrible " sweating-sickness " visited England for the last time. The witty French ambassador (Du Bellay, Bishop of Bayonne) gives us a vivid picture of Henry's uneasiness during the plague. He at once sent Anne Bullen to her father's house at Hever, and then, with the queen and Court, moved about from place to place for fear of infection, " confessing every day, and communicating on great feasts."

Thus Henry, while the Court laughed in its sleeve, and fresh, frantic efforts were being made to move earth—as heaven seemed impregnable—to secure the divorce.

Into the long and complicated political, social and religious questions of Henry VIII.'s divorce we cannot enter here ; but it is necessary, in writing the life of the future cardinal-legate to outline clearly the main facts of that appalling sin and scandal which changed Pole's whole career, and was the lever by which the temporal power of the Church was overthrown in England and the authority of the Holy See set aside ; while the king took the place of the Pope as Supreme Head of the Church in this country.

On May 31, 1529, the commission appointed by the Pope to sift thoroughly the details of Queen Katherine's first and second marriages, met at Blackfriars, under the two cardinal-legates, Wolsey and Campeggio ; and was in session until July 23. Eight or nine sittings were held, during one of which the cause of the queen was nobly and eloquently defended by Blessed John Fisher ; but nothing was effected, and Clement VII. summoned the case to Rome. Wolsey had failed to carry out the king's wishes, and from that moment his downfall was secure. " The fall of Wolsey," says a modern writer,* " was only delayed till Henry assured himself that his old minister's ruin was more profitable than his future service." He was stripped of his dignities and offices, and Sir Thomas More was made Lord Chancellor. " My Lord of Norfolk," writes the French ambassador, " is become president of the Council : my Lord of Suffolk vice-president : and above them both is Mistress Anne ! "

* A. Galton. "Character and Times of Thomas Cromwell," p. 43.

Pole, horrified at the turn affairs were taking, sought and obtained permission from the king in the autumn of 1529 to take up his residence at the University of Paris, to pursue his studies in theology. Here at least he would be free from the sordid vulgarity of Court intrigue, and there was little use in his remaining in England if the king would not listen to such advisers as Sir Thomas More and the Bishop of Rochester.

A month after Pole's arrival in Paris Cromwell (who had managed most successfully to exchange the service of the disgraced cardinal for that of the king) counselled Henry plainly to take over the supremacy of the Church. Little, it was clear, could be expected from the Pope; indeed it seemed certain that he would never declare Katherine's marriage with Henry to have been null and void from the beginning— the only possible means by which he could ever hope to marry Anne Bullen. Why not, therefore, simplify matters by substituting himself as supreme judge ? " England," remarked the minister, " is a monster with two heads "—a suggestion which might fairly be left to a monarch of Henry VIII.'s taste for capital punishment. On November 3, 1529, the Parliament " for the enormities of the clergy" assembled, heard High Mass of the Holy Ghost, and proceeded to debate. The king was present; Audley was speaker; Cromwell sat as member for Taunton ; and the new Lord Chancellor (who did not survive this Parliament) opened the session with a brilliant, ironical speech, construed by his enemies into a bitter attack upon Wolsey—which it was not. In this Parliament the schismatic suggestion of Cromwell —now chief secretary—was first breathed abroad ; and caused a thrill of horror.

Pole had not been long in Paris before he was, to use his own expression, " thunderstruck " to receive a message from Henry requesting him to obtain the decision of the Sorbonne as to the " legality " of his first marriage. This was, of course, the direct fruit of a suggestion by one Thomas Cranmer, then a private tutor at Cambridge, to the effect that a consensus of opinion should be taken from the European universities * on the question of the divorce ;—

* The universities consulted were those of France, which yielded to threats; N. Italy, which was bribed; and Protestant Germany. The Lutheran divines were

a suggestion to which he owed certainly his archbishopric, and presumably, his soul.

Pole, who had exiled himself to avoid the royal scandal, quietly resolved to ignore this request. Henry evidently chose to consider him as a kind of chief commissioner in his interests, and sent over the Bishop of Bayonne as his coadjutor. But on that prelate's arrival he was gently but definitely given to understand by Pole that the whole affair was in his—the ambassador's—hands, and must be concluded independently of himself; and that he could not allow his name to be associated in any way with the verdict of the university.

Protestant historians are filled with astonishment that at this juncture Queen Katherine did not do what to them seems the right and natural thing, and quietly step aside, leaving her husband free to wed in rapid succession, his remaining five wives; instead of opposing the divorce with all the strong political interest at her command. They argue that all love for such a man must

not unnaturally opposed to the "Defender of the Faith." Spain, Austria and the Low Countries were not consulted. Cambridge temporised. Oxford, a "Queen's City," only yielded to a direct threat of violence from the king, in 1530.

long ago have ceased, and that a separation on any terms must have been far more agreeable than to live as his wife with a man who caused her nothing but the most intense suffering. Nor do they ever grasp the fact that the sacrament of matrimony being indissoluble no such thing as divorce—in the Protestant sense of the word—is, or ever has been, recognised by the Catholic Church. It is, of course, true that in some cases marriages are annulled, even after a long lapse of years, upon the simple fact that they have never really been marriages at all ; owing to some informality or obstacle, such as kinship or affinity wilfully concealed, a previous unacknowledged marriage on the part of husband or wife, or the fact that one of the contracting parties was compelled by fear, or force. The invalidation of his marriage was exactly what the king was aiming at. But even if Katherine had actually lived with his brother as his wife, Clement VII. would doubtless not have annulled her subsequent marriage with Henry. Julius II. had especially provided in the dispensation for this contingency, though as a matter of fact—which the king moved heaven and earth in vain to disprove

—her first marriage had never been anything but a formal contract, owing to the ill-health of Prince Arthur.

Upon these facts, with which Pole was perfectly acquainted, the whole question turned.

On November 29, 1530, Cardinal Wolsey died—an event which Anne Bullen's father celebrated by a magnificent banquet and entertainment to the king; at which was performed a realistic play representing the cardinal's descent into hell, and his reception there. At Henry's command Pole returned to England, to his retreat at Sheen, and was at once offered the Archbishopric of York, by the king. " There was no obstacle," said Henry, " to his accepting it, except . . . that (insignificant) matter of the divorce."

It was, perhaps, the crisis of Reginald Pole's life. The king did not hesitate to tamper with the young man's family; promising them riches—and what was far more valuable, personal security—if only Pole would accept . . . the bribe ! It was a mere question of policy, he remarked ; in fact, the reason he wanted Pole to be archbishop was that he might always be guided by his advice in spiritual matters.

The Duke of Norfolk was sent to intercede with him ; he was told that York and Winchester would both be kept open for three months, and he might accept either. The revenues were vast ; the king was anxious to secure Pole by any means ; his family implored him ; the dazzling prospect of a career equal to that of Wolsey, but marred by none of that prelate's mistakes, lay before him. He told the king at last that he would take a month to consider. It is evident he scarcely knew what to say, for there is no doubt that he hoped, as archbishop, to be able to stem effectually the steadily rising tide of schism which now threatened England.

In the meantime Parliament met, on January 3, 1531, and Convocation assembled at Westminster eighteen days later. Clearly and definitely now, Henry demanded the title of Supreme Head of the Church, and sought to compass his end by involving both assemblies under the Statute of Præmunire, by which their liberty and entire possessions were forfeited to the crown. Terrified beyond measure, Convocation offered a " spontaneous oblation " of nearly a million pounds, current value, to escape what they too clearly foresaw. This was exactly what Henry wanted. He refused to accept the gift unless the bishops and clergy would accept him as Supreme Head of the Church. It was an awful moment. "The clergy," says a Protestant historian,* "had defied the lion, and the lion held them in his grasp ; and they could but struggle helplessly, supplicate, and submit."

On February 9 a royal message was sent to know if Henry's terms were accepted ; and a futile attempt was made to soften Cromwell, and later on, the king. Henry refused to see the deputation. Then they knew it was all or nothing ; Pope or king, life or death. But schism . . . and open rupture with the Church universal . . . they dared not risk it ! Better, after all, to lose their lives than their souls. The king, privately advised that they were "stubborn," made a significant concession. The admission now ran :

"Ecclesiæ et cleri Anglicani singularem protectorem et unicum et supremum Dominum, *et quantum per lege Christi licet*, etiam supremum caput ipsius Majestatem agnoscimus." ("We acknowledge his Majesty

* Froude. Vol. i. 298.

as the only protector, as the sole and sovereign lord, *and as far as the law of Christ allows*, even as the Supreme Head of the Church and Clergy of England.")

On February 11, this amendment, read by the aged Archbishop Warham, passed in sullen, furious silence. At a later session Convocation discussed it, and nearly all declared they had saved their consciences. Henry accepted the "spontaneous oblation" with dignity; dismissed Convocation; granted the "pardon" (which the Commons, only just in time, discovered did not include themselves); and before Parliament was prorogued on March 31, 1531, the Lords had sent to the Pope a letter instructing him as to his duties, and detailing at some length the merits of the divorce.

There was not much doubt as to what Pole's answer would be, now. Henry sent for him to Greenwich palace in the firm conviction that he would accept the Archbishopric. But the moment they came face to face the Spirit of God seemed to descend upon the future Cardinal, and for the first time for many years Henry VIII. listened to the truth from the lips of one whom he respected in spite of himself. All Pole's doubt and hesitation were gone; he felt no fear of the great passionate man, who walked up and down the long gallery, fingering his dagger, with which, he afterwards declared, he was strongly tempted to stab the speaker. Nothing, he confessed, but his fearlessness and simplicity saved Pole, who spoke as one delivering a message from God; and who afterwards drew up his reasons for declining the dignity in a letter to the King which caused Henry to say his cousin had added insult to injury; though he retracted this later, and certainly respected Pole more than ever.

But the definite step was taken; he had made his great refusal; privately, at least he had made an enemy of the King, and the King was supreme now. Only exile remained—he must leave England without loss of time.

But if he had sacrificed his brilliant future at least he had not sacrificed his soul.

CHAPTER III

THE CHALLENGE AND THE ANSWER
1531–1536

REGINALD POLE spent the first year of his exile at Avignon, a town directly under the jurisdiction of the Pope, and at a safer distance from England than Paris. Here, however, he found the winter so cold and bleak that he decided upon returning to Padua, and the sunnier skies of Italy. In 1532 he set out for his old University by way of Carpentras, where he remained some time as the guest of the bishop, Monseigneur Sadolet, a well-known man of letters, who was charmed with him. All through his life Pole seems to have possessed a unique gift for making and keeping friends, for which he may well be envied, and which he largely owed to his unselfishness and deep humility. Sadolet wrote to Ghiberti, Bishop of Verona, whose friendship Pole renewed on the next stage of his journey, telling him how he had enjoyed Pole's too short visit, and how they had discussed literature, and plans of study, comparing notes—the elder man asking for and acting upon the advice of the younger. " I find him," said the new friend to the old, " a genius of the first class ; with a consummate knowledge of the Greek and Latin languages, . . . and with great elegance of manners."

At Padua Pole at once set about forming a household on his former lines ; one member of which was his old friend Bonamico. He made the acquaintance of Cosmo Gherio, the future Bishop of Fano, and of Beccadelli, his biographer and life-long friend, also a member of his household. Again he gave himself unreservedly to the dear delight of study, and almost forgot his troubles. This was his true environment—here he was happy—surrounded by his friends, his books, in a great peaceful house where the sweet, silent, solitary hours alternated with brilliant debate in the senate-house, and not less brilliant conversation with the greatest scholars and thinkers of Europe, most of whom were his own personal friends. Many were the visits he paid to Venice, the home of his two great friends, Bembo, and

Aloysius Priuli. Together they planned expeditions to the distant islands across the lovely lagoon ; and explored the wonders of the City in the Sea—the magical beauty of San Marco ; San Giovanni è Paulo of the Dominicans, where the Doges lie in solemn state ; and all the treasured riches of the glorious Venetian churches.

At the mouth of the wide Giudecca Canal stands, on a small island, the great Benedictine monastery of San Giorgio, with its famous campanile ; and this place was a favourite resort of Pole's, who had formed a warm friendship with the abbot, Don Gregorio Cortesio, a learned and saintly man ; and also with a religious of the order, Don Marco. Of the latter, Pole, writing five years later, said : " There is no one to whom I more readily listen, discoursing on divinity."* In a letter to Cardinal Contarini at Rome—a friend of his university life—he says : " Venice is Eden, and we only want you to make a fourth." He revelled in the beauty by which he was surrounded, particularly in the wonderful Venetian gardens ; such as that of the old Palazzo Bembo, on a waterway between

* August 10, 1536.

the Grand Canal and the Giudecca ; in which even at noon the black ilexes and yews make a cool retreat of the narrow shrubbery where a tiny brook trickles and tinkles over the mossy stones, below a fern-fringed winding walk ; while through the green dimness dazzling masses of flowers riot under a burning sun.

At Venice, too, Pole first met Caraffa, the founder of the Theatines, the fiery Neapolitan who was to become Pope Paul IV. ; the man who was first his friend, then his rival, and who ended by breaking his heart.

Perhaps these four years, taken alto-gether, are the happiest of Reginald Pole's life. But it says much for his strength of character that in spite of all his friends, of his easy circumstances, (for the King still continued his allowance as Pole had not publicly declared himself his enemy), and the temptations to idleness of all kinds by which he was surrounded, he never gave up his systematic course of study, and that his reputation as one of the fore-most scholars of the university steadily increased.

Meanwhile in England the logical conse-

Henry VIII.

quence of the events of 1531 had come to pass. On January 15, 1534, Parliament met and entered upon the final stage of the separation of England from the church universal. To the King, it enacted, were to belong all the jurisdiction and offices of the Pope in England, and—what was at least as important to Henry—all the tithes and offerings belonging to the Holy See. Peter's Pence were abolished, Annates made payable to the King, also a yearly tithe on all clerical incomes. The bishops were required to swear that they " abjured the Pope." It was made treason to speak against Henry or Anne, or to call the former infidel, tyrant, heretic or schismatic—no doubt a wise precaution !

The statute concluded by asserting that the country was not separating from Catholic Unity, but only from the Papacy. How the King differentiated between the Catholic Church and its Visible Head was not stated. This also was prudent, as Henry continued to proclaim himself a " good Catholic." Shortly after, an Act was passed cutting off the Princess Mary from the succession and requiring from the nation an oath of allegiance to Elizabeth, daughter of Anne

Bullen ; and a recognition of the King's "marriage" with that lady, which had taken place on January 25, 1533.

On November 3, 1534, Parliament reassembled, and on the 4th the act was finally passed which distinctly and definitely cut the last link. The Supreme Headship of the Church of England was conferred absolutely on the King. " Be it enacted," says the statute, " that the King our Sovereign Lord, his heirs and successors, kings of this realm, shall be taken, accepted, and reputed as the only Supreme Head in earth of the Church of England, called *Anglicana Ecclesia*."* This act was followed by another making it high treason to deny the Royal Supremacy in the King or his heirs.

The blow had fallen ! Catholic England had been deliberately driven into the dreary darkness of schism by the furious passions and ungovernable will of one unhappy man. The honour of heading the glorious roll of martyrs who sealed the truth with their blood belongs to the three Carthusian Priors, who, with two other priests, on May 4, 1535, were butchered at Tyburn for denying the

* Act of Supremacy.   26 Henry VIII. cap. 1.

King's Supremacy, and refusing to take the oath ; and who, dying, gave God glory that they were counted worthy to suffer for his name. Sir Thomas More and Bishop Fisher, who had just been created cardinal, were already in the tower for the same cause. On June 19, three more Carthusians suffered. Three days later, on June 22, the aged Bishop of Rochester, Blessed John Fisher, King Henry's former tutor, was beheaded on Tower Hill; and on July 6, Blessed Thomas More, Lord High Chancellor of England, suffered there for the same " crime."

All Europe thrilled and sickened at the savage barbarity. " God is my witness," said Pole, writing of the death of More, " that involuntary tears fall from my eyes which blot out what I have written, and almost hinder me from going on with the subject." The horrible murders were not an outrage to the Holy See only, but to the whole civilised world. But the end was not yet.

During the early part of 1535, shortly after his assumption of the title of " Supreme Head " Henry, who had been sounding Thomas Starkey (now his chaplain) as to

Pole's probable attitude, wrote himself to his cousin requiring his opinion on this proceeding, and on the divorce; sending him a treatise upon the subject, by Sampson, Bishop of Chichester. Starkey also wrote advising Pole how to answer. "Fearlessly," he said, "state your opinion. So you will honour God's truth and satisfy the King, who lately said to me: He would rather you were buried there than you should for any worldly promotion or profit to yourself dissemble with him in these great and weighty causes." Pole was at Ravelone, near Venice, the country seat of Priuli, whose guest he was when these epistles reached him. He at once sent Henry's letter to his wisest and most influential adviser, Cardinal Contarini, then at Rome; who said of it that the arguments were futile and weak, but arranged with much skill.

In his famous "letter" to the Emperor Charles V. written some years later, Pole says that these questions were precisely those to avoid which he had exiled himself; for had he agreed with them he must have been a traitor to the King's honour, his own conviction, and the welfare of his country. He had hitherto kept silence, though many thought he should have spoken out. But Henry—characteristically—had waited till it was death to oppose him, and then asked for his opinion. "His orders were that I should send him my opinion in terms so clear and explicit as to avoid all ambiguity and subterfuge ; and if I failed in so doing that I should incur his highest displeasure." Fisher and More had been quoted to terrify him, but : "I saw (in their deaths) the strongest motives to support with an unshaken resolution the cause for which they had laid down their lives." He goes on to say that he would rather renounce everything than compromise with the King, and what strengthened him most in this attitude was the blood of the martyrs. "That divine truth has always so manifested itself we are assured, first by His death who was very truth. . . . . . . These considerations banish all my dread, arm me with generous confidence, and give me to understand what are the true objects of fear and hope."* He decided to answer

* Apol. R. Poli ad Carolum Caes : super quatuor libris a se scriptis : " *De Unitate Ecclesiæ.*" (No. 2, *et seq.*)

Henry's questions at length. On April 12, 1535, Harvel, the English ambassador at Venice, writes to Starkey that he will try to influence Pole as the King wishes, and make him return to his native country, but that " he [Pole] delights more in study than in life or glory, which has always been contemned by him." He consumes " his perpetual life at letters." " It is true that the sweetness of learning is so great that with difficulty a man greatly inflamed with virtue can be withdrawn from study, but between you and me and others, I hope we shall remove him from that ardent mind without any dubitation." * Starkey's opinion of Pole, written about the same time to Cromwell, in connection with his expected answer to the King's message, is : " There lives not a more sincere man on earth than Master Pole, and whatever he thinks in these causes the King will be sure to know shortly." †

Harvel, writing again to Starkey on April 21 says : " The performing of [Mr. Pole's] book will somewhat slake him, for his study is too fervent in that work. It will be an

* " Letters and Papers of Henry VIII.," ix., (i.) 535.
† *Ibid.* ix., (i.) 575.

able monument of his wit and virtue. The greatest discomfort he could have would be to leave it imperfect, which he thinks he would do if he did not finish it in this quiet life." *

Pole was indeed working hard at his reply at Venice, and the greater part was probably written among his Benedictine friends at San Giorgio.

In May, Starkey, who was exceedingly anxious as to the nature of his friend's answer, wrote to him : " I am glad to see, by the few words you wrote, that you will apply yourself to satisfy the King's request, which was, in few words, clearly and plainly without colour or cloak of dissimulation to shew your sentence in his lately defined cause. This I am sure you will do gladly, for you will not dissemble with a King, from which dissimulation I have never seen a mind more abhorring ! " He describes at great length the death of the Carthusians, referring to them as persons " who, as much as in them lay, have rooted sedition in the community ; " and ends by expressing Henry's wonder that Pole should prefer a retired and scholastic life ; and by a fine

* " Letters and Papers of Henry VIII.," ix. (i.) 579.

dose of flattery as to that monarch's intentions towards him.* Starkey's view of the Carthusian martyrdoms, however, was scarcely that of his friends abroad, for Harvel tells him, in a letter dated June 15, that they were " considered here to be of extreme cruelty, and all Venice was in great murmuration to hear it . . .they consider their execution as against all honest laws of God and man . . . I never saw Italians break out so vehemently at anything."†

Pole seems to have reassured the King's chaplain as to the fact of his writing a reply for : " I did not doubt of your will," writes Starkey, "but your long silence made me fear that the cause little liked you."

In August, 1535, we hear of Pole in Venice, befriending a certain Moryson, a poor scholar and notorious beggar, whose books and even his clothes had been seized for debt by the Jews. Writing to Starkey, Moryson says that he is now wearing the livery of Mr. Michael Throgmorton, Signor Polo's servant, and that his master's kindness had rescued him from " misery . . .

* " Letters and Papers of Henry VIII.," ix., (i.) 801,
† *Ibid.* ix. (i.) 874.

hunger, cold and poverty . . . I shall love him," he adds, "as long as God gives me life;"* a sentiment which did not however prevent this estimable man from writing next year of "Mr. Traitor Pole."†

An amusing letter from Pole's butler, Sandro, to Starkey from Venice (October 1, 1535), informs us that Priuli "is as much in love with my lord as ever . . . while we were at Sta. Croce he came to stay there, and never ceased till he drew Il Signore to his house at Padua."‡ "It is expensive enough to keep house here," he adds feelingly; "but much more to move about . . . The Bishop of Verona (Ghiberti) sent the other day to Il Signore 250 gold crowns, praying him to accept them to buy horses to visit him at Verona. Il Signore has sent them back, promising to go and stay a few days with him."§ Three weeks later Sandro says: "We have a fine house on

* "Letters and Papers of HenryVIII.," ix. (ii.) 101–2.
† *Ibid.* xi. 1481.
‡ This butler was, he tells us, "writing a book of Basilio," by Pole's desire, "which is almost printed" and which he was "collating . . . with texts in St. Mark's library"—evidently an unusual sort of servant.
§ "Letters and Papers of Henry VIII.," ix. (ii.) 512.

the Grand Canal, between the house of Foscari and the ferry of St. Barnabas ; " and speaking of a friend of Pole's : " His present house is so small and cold and foul that it drove away Il Signore."

But the most delightful account of Pole which we have from Venice is in a letter to Starkey on December 1 from one John Friar. " Pole is studying divinity, and . . . despising things merely human and terrestrial. He is undergoing a great change, exchanging man for God." *

By this time Henry's request had become publicly known, and Pole's answer was eagerly looked for. " The King," says Chapuys, the Imperial ambassador in England, on December 15, " has written expressly to Reginald Pole who is at Venice, to send him his opinion in writing *de primatu pontificis.* Would that the King had done it to hear the simple truth, and not to have a pretext for injuring Pole, who is one of the most virtuous persons in the world, and who will do a great deal when there is any talk of putting affairs here right ; " † a prophecy most literally fulfilled.

---

* " Letters and Papers of Henry VIII.," ix. (ii.) dated Dec. 1535. † *Ibid.* ix. (ii.) 988.

" Master Pole," writes Harvel at Venice, " is in vehement study of writing to satisfy the King,"* and on December 28, 1535, he adds : " he is writing to the King . . . a fair work which will be *æternum monumentum et ingenii et virtutis suæ*. He keeps it secret to himself, for he wishes the King to be the first reader."† And again, on January 18, of the next year : " Mr. Pole is continual in writing of his work, and that with extreme study, which breaketh him much, especially in these sharp colds which have reigned many days."‡

This was the great treatise which was to set Christendom on fire, Pole's masterpiece, *De Unitate Ecclesiæ*. It was divided into four parts. In the first the writer boldly refutes the error of the King in proclaiming himself head of the Church of England ; rebukes him for the sin of schism ; and makes short work of Bishop Sampson's treatise on the matter. In the second, he declares the Supremacy of the Apostolic See of Rome over the whole world, and answers objections. The third book is a solemn warning, remind-

* " Letters and Papers of Henry VIII.," ix. (ii.) 927.
† *Ibid.* ix. (ii.) 1029.
‡ *Ibid.* x. (Jan. 1536).

D

ing the King of the righteous blood he has shed, for which retribution would certainly be required in this life as well as in the next ; and speaking plainly of the temporal punishment which would probably befall him from the Catholic Sovereigns if he persisted in his madness.   In the fourth, Pole apologises frankly if he has said too much, or spoken too strongly, begging him to believe that every word proceeded from the highest motives of zeal and affection.

It was a manly, courageous piece of work, but when it was finished the writer paused. Before sending it to Henry he submitted it to Cardinal Contarini, begging him to read it " like an enemy and not a friend,"* and to Priuli.   Both at first were of opinion that Pole had gone too far, and that if the King read the treatise nothing would prevent him from wreaking vengeance on its author.   Contarini recommended milder words.   Pole replied that strong language is sometimes necessary, and that he had never found that temporising did any good. "Flattery," he writes from Venice, on March 4, 1536, " has been the cause of all the evil."   However, he added, if his

* " Letters and Papers of Henry VIII." x. 217.

friends were still of the same opinion when they had read the whole carefully, he would make the alterations they recommended.

To Priuli Pole wrote that it was utterly against his nature to blame the King, but that Henry could not possibly succeed unless he was aware of his own failures ; and that from his own close relationship and the fact that Henry had pointedly and directly appealed to him to do so, no one could point out those failures with greater right than he. There was no sacrifice, he said, which he could not make to promote the King's happiness, which he set above all earthly considerations. He warns Priuli, however, of the danger of treating Henry with anything but firmness. " Soft words are of no use, for gentleness and dissimulation have driven him to this madness." *
Lenity he mistook for cowardice : " misplaced softness has cast him into an abyss of exemplary vice ; " and in this opinion a historian of very different calibre—the agnostic Hume—will be found to uphold the author of *De Unitate Ecclesiæ*.

The work was eventually printed without alteration. Priuli begged that Contarini

* Poli Epist. I. 437.

might show the treatise to the Pope, but Pole refused, as in the present highly strained state of affairs Henry would not unnaturally be very angry if the treatise, addressed to himself, were first read by the Holy Father.

He spent Easter at Padua; and there followed a few weeks of anxious delay, caused by the dread of the vengeance which Henry would certainly take on Pole's family. However, in May, 1536, the news of Anne Bullen's execution decided him to send his treatise to the King at once.

Five months earlier, on January 8 of the same year, the tragedy of the life of Katherine of Aragon had closed. Like her daughter Mary, she passed away while hearing and answering the Mass which was being said near her deathbed—her last act, to receive Viaticum.

Her death was celebrated by a great feast, at which Henry rejoiced publicly, brilliantly clad in yellow. On the day of the funeral a dead son was born to the dead woman's husband and Anne Bullen. Disappointed of an heir, and weary of the woman for whom he had sold his soul, Henry found no difficulty of any kind in disposing of her. Hideous charges were brought against her. She was tried ; condemned, with five men ; and executed on May 19, 1536. Henry spent that day with one of her ladies-in-waiting, Jane Seymour, to whom he was betrothed on May 20, and whom he married ten days later, by a special " dispensation " from Cranmer—now Archbishop of Canterbury—granted on the very day of Anne Bullen's execution.

Pole wrote to a friend that the death of Anne Bullen would mean one of two things : either that the King would repent and submit ; or that he would harden his heart, and be lost. On May 27, 1536, directly the news reached him, he dispatched his treatise by the hand of his trusted servant, Michael Throgmorton, from Venice, commending it earnestly to God. It was delivered to Henry by Sir John Russell, a gentleman of the King's Privy Chamber. Henry received it eagerly, glanced through it, and sent back Throgmorton post-haste to Venice to command Pole's instant attendance at court, in order to " explain certain difficulties " which, he said, occurred to him, immediately !

This invitation Pole declined, besides an even more pressing one from Cromwell.

" I despair of England," * he wrote to Contarini, on June 8. With a certain quiet humour he remarks in the " letter " to the Emperor that he was wily enough to see " like the cautious animal in the fable " the footprints of those creatures which had gone into the lion's den ; but not one of those which had returned ! †

He wrote a polite refusal to the King, explaining that he had expressed himself in language too simple and clear to be misunderstood. But Henry had not yet received this when another royal express arrived at Venice with letters from Cromwell and Bishop Tunstall of Durham ; the latter refuting Pole's treatise—which he had not read—and Cromwell (who in 1535 had been created Vicar-General and held a stall in Salisbury Cathedral; and was now, as Lord Privy Seal and Vicegerent of the King, presiding in Convocation and taking precedence of the Archbishop), taking it for granted that Pole was on his way to England, and informing him of the change in Tunstall's views ; a prelate, he added, of whom Pole had always thought highly. Lest their

* " Letters and Papers of Henry VIII." x. 1093.

† Apol. ad Car. Caes., tom. i. ep. xli. R. Poli.

meeting should cause Pole " shyness and surprise," the great man thought well to warn him of his change of front, for the avoiding of " uneasiness."

Henry, foreseeing that Pole would probably not return at the first summons, wrote through Tunstall that he would allow him to remain abroad on condition that he would destroy all that he had written; and promise to write no more against the King and his edicts, under a signed and sealed engagement.* Tunstall's letter, wrote Pole, was rather a volume than an epistle.

This prelate had taunted Pole with the benefits he had received from Henry's hands, and the education he owed to the King. To this Pole replied that no benefits, whatever gratitude he might feel to their giver, could buy his conscience; and he came at once to close quarters with Tunstall by adding that argument between them was useless, as they had not the common ground of obedience to the Holy See. " My zeal for his Majesty," he adds with dignity, " shall be the return which I make to him for my education . . . and above all, of what I owe to my own character as a Christian."

* Ep. R. Poli ad Ed. VI. Ang. Reg. Cap. 25.

To his mother he wrote, on July 15, 1536, a most touching letter, full of the deepest tenderness, begging her not to "greve" that he could not return home. "Remember," he added, "that ever you had given me utterly unto God. And though you had so done with all your children, yet in me you had so given all right from you . . . that you never took any care to provide for my living . . . but committed all to God, to whom you had given me. This promise now, madam, in my Master's name I require of you to maintain . . . the which you cannot keep . . . if you now begin to care for me. When you see me complain of my Master, then . . . will it be time for you to care for me . . . so that if you will enjoy in me . . . any comfort . . . the readiest way is . . . to let me and my Master alone . . . knowing to what Master you have given me . . . (which) shall be to me the greatest comfort I can have of you." *

But these letters had not been sent when on July 19, 1536, an urgent message from Pope Paul III. summoned their writer to Rome.

* "Letters and Papers of Henry VIII." xi. (i.) 92.

CHAPTER IV

THE FIRST LEGATION

1536–1537

POPE PAUL III., who had for many years desired to bring about a thorough reformation of discipline in the Church, had finally decided to assemble a small, representative body of men at Rome with whom he could consult on the matter.

Those whom he invited were distinguished either for scholarship and brilliant literary achievements, or for eminent saintliness of life—in several cases for both. Though Reginald Pole was still young, and yet a layman, the Pope had heard too much of him from Cardinal Contarini * not to be anxious to secure his cool judgment and weighty advice on certain important and difficult questions.

But it was with very mingled feelings that

* Cardinal Contarini, in 1536, was created Bishop of Belluno, a beautiful province in the Dolomite country. (Cardella, v., p. 155.)

Pole received the Papal command. Besides his genuine humility he felt deep concern that the summons should come at the very moment when, by obeying it, he would seem to be definitely siding against Henry, who would not fail to misconstrue his action. He wrote a very careful letter to the King, informing him of the circumstances, and of his own surprise at the summons to Rome, enclosing a copy of the Pope's mandate. This he sent without delay, together with his letter to his mother, and the replies to Cromwell and Tunstall; earnestly hoping that the King would receive it before learning from a hostile source of the journey to Rome. On July 27, he wrote to the Pope, expressing his wonder at the call of one who had no other desire or expectation but to live " in a private station "; explaining how anxious he was to avoid unnecessarily wounding Henry's feelings, or rousing him to anger; and that his coming to Rome at the very moment when he had refused to present himself at the King's court could scarcely fail to do both; as Henry would certainly take it for granted that the visit to Rome was a political one. He adds that he cannot yet despair of Henry, however others may; and hopes England may be saved by the proposed Council.*

Pole left Venice at the end of September, 1536, with Caraffa, Archbishop of Chieti; the Abbot of San Giorgio, who was to have accompanied them having gone on in advance to visit the Bishop of Salerno, another member of the Council. At Verona Pole and Caraffa were joined by Bishop Ghiberti, and here an express post-haste from England very nearly stopped Pole's journey altogether. Michael Throgmorton brought him furious letters from Henry himself, as well as from Starkey, Cromwell and Tunstall, threatening dire penalties not only on himself but on his family should he persevere in his intention of going to Rome. Henry, with his usual astuteness, easily saw what a tremendously important political situation might be created were his determined cousin and the Pope to meet; and did not for a moment hesitate to threaten the lives of a number of innocent people in order to prevent the meeting . . . a pleasant method of elementary simplicity much affected by Henry!

Starkey wrote an angry but stately letter

* Epist. R. Poli, vol. i., p. 467.

—the last, he said, that Pole should ever receive from him, expressing his disappointment and disgust with *De Unitate*, and with the writer for making the test of Catholicity union with Rome. " More [and] Rochester . . . suffered by their own folly. They only died for a superstition, as, I think, no wise man shall do hereafter."*

These letters Pole might have disregarded, but there were others. His brother, Lord Montague, and his aged mother, both sent messages which must have been bitter to read. "Son Reginald," wrote Margaret Pole, " I send you God's blessing and mine, though my trust to have comfort in you is turned to sorrow. Alas, that I, through your folly, should receive such message as I have late done by your brother. To me . . . his Highness has shewn such mercy and pity as I could never deserve. . . . And now, to see you in his Grace's indignation. . . trust me, Reginald, there went never the death of thy father or of any child so nigh mine heart. Upon my blessing I charge thee to take another way, and serve our Master,† as thy duty is, unless thou

* " Letters and Papers of Henry VIII.," xi. (i.) 402.
† Henry.

wilt be the confusion of thy mother. You write of a promise made by you to God. Son, that was to serve God and thy prince, whom if thou do not serve with all thy wit, with all they power, I know thou cannot please God. I will pray God to give thee grace to serve thy prince truly, or else, to take thee to His mercy." *

"Gentle Reginald," wrote his eldest brother, whose fears were only too well grounded : "let no scrupulosity so embrace [you] but that we, which be so knit in nature, and so happily born under so noble a prince, may so join together to serve him as our bounden duty requireth. It is incredible to me that by reason of a brief sent you from the Bishop of Rome † you should be resident with him this winter. If you should take that way then farewell all my hope . . . and then farewell all bonds of nature. . . . But utterly without hope I cannot be . . . that you would so highly offend God . . . without the devil have so much power over you ; from the which to keep

* " Letters and Papers of Henry VIII.," xi. (ii.) 93.

† It was forbidden to speak of the Pope except as the Bishop of Rome, at the end of 1533.

you I shall as heartily pray as I would be a partner of the joys of Heaven." *

Reginald Pole's very soul was wrung with anguish. Again he stood at the parting of the ways. It was a small thing to be denounced by the King . . . but his own mother ! . . . All that was human in his soul ; patriotism, family honour, love . . . above all the unquenchable dread of the danger incurred by these helpless people— a danger which he was by his present action converting into a deadly certainty,—rose up within him, clamouring that he should give up the journey to Rome — insisting that he should yield. He asked himself in agony of spirit if he were not called upon, at least for the sake of those others, to obey his King's command—after all a merely negative one, and to plead the letters he had just received as an excuse to the Pope, who would surely understand that as a member of the English royal family he could scarcely be called upon to take a prominent part in any scheme of papal policy.

And, on the other hand, there was the definite call of the Vicar of Christ to work

* "Letters and Papers of Henry VIII.," dated September 13, 1536., xi. (i.) 451.

which he knew was not political ; and he knew, too, that nothing in the world was an excuse for refusing that call. He consulted Caraffa and Ghiberti. Very tenderly they reminded him that spiritual authority must come before temporal—had he not written in defence of that very principle himself, and could he lose so glorious an opportunity of vindicating it ? There was no doubt at all as to what he ought to do. And so, after a struggle, of the bitterness of which we dare not think, Pole decided. To Contarini he wrote that the letters from his brother and mother, " written in a miserable strain," had touched him so deeply that he had nearly succumbed.* To his mother he wrote a letter full of tenderness, reminding her of his duty to God, rather than man ; begging her to believe that he had acted according to his conscience, and that he could not do otherwise. He told Cromwell that his threats did not terrify him ; and patiently explained Tunstall's difficulties, writing to each in terms which could not be mistaken.†

* " Letters and Papers of Henry VIII.," xi. (ii.), 256.

† Epist. R. Poli, pars. 1a, p. 470.

He kept the courier with him until he and his friends reached Bologna, and then despatched him to England with a heart which must have ached in spite of his courage. The King was now openly defied, and there was no doubt that he would do his worst.

But his companions, and indeed, the whole papal court were deeply impressed with the significance of what had passed ; and the importance of the man who, seeking nothing but peace and retirement, was the object of continual overtures on the part of such a King as Henry VIII. Pole himself wrote to Contarini from Siena that now they despaired of securing him by persuasion, they would not hesitate to employ force . . . a prophecy most literally fulfilled.

Every honour was paid to the young Englishman when the party reached Rome. He was lodged in the Vatican, and was deeply touched by the kindness he received. Of the nine Commissioners, all but the Arch-bishop of Salerno were his personal friends ; and five had been his fellow travellers. Cardinal Contarini, a wise and saintly prelate, was president of the Commission, which had, broadly speaking, to put into practical working form various theories of the Holy Father on matters of discipline, and the interior government of the Church. Contarini laid the subjects in order before the Council, requesting every one to give his opinion on each question, in writing ; but Cortesio begged Pole, who was the great Cardinal's intimate friend, to request him to allow each man to take a different subject for though, as an old biographer* delightfully puts it : " the candour of all . . . was such that they would judge of each other's performances . . . with perhaps greater impartiality than their own," still, so as not to break perfect unity, it was deemed advisable to adopt Cortesio's suggestion. An eloquent Dominican Cardinal, comprehending more clearly than the others the vastness of the reforms involved, begged the Holy Father to postpone their discussion to a General Council ; and this, in fact, was done a few years later at the Council of Trent.

Meantime it was evident that Pole, though by far the youngest member of the Council, was by no means the least practical ; and his opinion was sought by all. It was

* Beccadelli.

indeed to him that the plan of reformation was finally entrusted, and published later in his name alone, without those of any coadjutors.

The Pope was deeply interested in the question of the reform of the lives of the clergy and, of all the subjects laid before the Council, he had this most at heart. Keenly alive to the importance of the influence of the Sacred College, he was determined to fill up its ranks with none but men of saintly and blameless character, who could be trusted to carry out his principles of reform. There were several vacancies to be filled at the next Consistory, and the Pope had from the first determined that Reginald Pole should be one of the new Cardinals. Beccadelli, (afterwards Archbishop of Ragusa) Pole's friend and biographer, who had accompanied him to Rome, tells us that, as he was still a layman, many had considered it possible that he should eventually marry the Princess Mary—an alliance at one time contemplated by her father, Henry VIII.—as he had been her friend from childhood, his mother having been appointed as her governess and chief lady-in-waiting by the King and Queen. The two had not met for years, and there is not a particle of evidence to prove that Pole had thought of marriage, even with Mary Tudor, for a moment. Still, it was generally felt that his elevation to the rank of Cardinal would effectually silence these suspicions.

Pole, however, was deeply distressed when the Pope's intentions became evident, and earnestly begged the Holy Father to consider that Henry could not fail to believe that Pole had known all the time the true reason of his summons to Rome, and had defied him, secure in the knowledge of the Pope's protection and the dazzling prospect of the Cardinalate.

Paul III. was moved by his passionate protest, and promised, says Beccadelli, to strike his name off the list of Cardinals-elect—to Pole's intense relief and gratitude. However, on the very morning of the Consistory, the Holy Father, having deeply considered the question, sent abruptly for Pole, whose dismay was indescribable; but, finding the Pope absolutely determined, he surrendered himself "like a sheep into the hands of her shearers," says his friend, who was present. He received the tonsure, and was with twelve others, amongst whom were his friends Sadolet and Caraffa, created

Cardinal on December 22, 1536, under the title of SS. Nereus and Achilleus. A few days later came a despatch from certain of the Catholics in England, praying the Pope to create him Cardinal, and to send him as Papal legate to his native country. This also came to pass ; for on February 7, 1537, he was created Legate *de latere* to England. His appointment, it was felt, would keep up the courage of those who were fighting to the death, for their faith ; and Pole himself, fearless now that the step was once taken, burned with enthusiasm to reconcile King Henry VIII.* He remembered, he tells us, that he was now a successor of the Apostles, whose blood had been shed for the Church ; the very crimson and scarlet of his Cardinal's robes reminded him of the martyrs in whose footsteps he, too, was called to tread and, it might well be, to give his life as they had given theirs : " as, having the same cause in common . . . I may hope to have the same Protector, and be entitled to the same reward." He was now a Prince of the Church, and his Cardinalate was everywhere looked upon as a certain pledge of the promised ecclesiastical reformation.

* Epist. R. Poli, pars. 1a., p. 55.

Among the dozens of letters of congratulation which he received, not one was from his own country, and this caused him bitter grief—but one from the Doge of Venice must have encouraged him greatly. The writer says that he and all Venice rejoiced at the news ; and that the whole of Christendom is indebted to the Pope for the new Cardinal ; and that as he could not possibly say all he felt in a letter he had instructed his ambassador to wait upon Pole, and tell him all that was in his—the Doge's—heart. Pole replied that Venice, his second home, was dearer to him than perhaps any other city, except Padua ; and at the close of a most grateful letter tells the Doge that he has a right to consider him as a Venetian subject.

Meantime there were many obstacles in the way of his mission to England. His instructions were to keep in touch with the Northern Catholics, who, goaded to madness, had just attempted a rising in Yorkshire. The Legate was to encourage them, and, if it was impossible to cross to England, to remain as near as possible—in France, or on the coast of Flanders.

England was indeed in a pitiable plight.

The last year, 1536, had seen the dissolution of all the smaller religious houses, and most of the greater ones ; while at the present time Cromwell's tools, Legh and Layton, were proceeding with their second "visitation" of the remainder. When the new Parliament met on June 9, there was a new Queen ; and Anne's marriage had to be declared null and void, and her daughter Elizabeth proclaimed illegitimate, as of course she was. Convocation, assembling at the same time, had to listen to a sermon from Latimer in which he roundly abused that time-serving body, and inveighed furiously against relics, images, purgatory and the Saints. Convocation, not unnaturally, was neither flattered nor edified, but by its own act, it was powerless to check heresy, and Protestantism had been spreading widely since Wolsey's death.

Under the Vicegerent Cromwell's direction, it passed a *Confession of Faith*, in which the Bible, the three Creeds, and the first four general Councils were mentioned as the general grounds of belief. Three Sacraments—Baptism, Penance, and the Holy Eucharist—were referred to as worthy of acceptance ; and the *Confession* upheld the doctrine of the Real Presence. Saints in general, it was announced, might be invoked with advantage ; but not individual saints—a slightly illogical tenet for which, prudently, no explanation was offered. " Superstition " was to be discouraged, and, no doubt to this end, a copy of the Bible in Latin and English was ordered to be set up in every parish church by August 1, the Feast of St. Peter in Chains.

Discontent, ever smouldering, burst into fierce flame in Yorkshire and Lincolnshire ; and at Louth, on October 1, 1536, a general rising took place ; the people clamouring for the abolition of the Protestant bishops, and the restitution of the ancient order, particularly of the monasteries ; and claiming their right to seven sacraments. The Northern peers, ready to die for their faith, were in communication with the Pope and the powerful Emperor Charles V. A Catholic alliance was planned between the Emperor, Francis I. of France, and James V. of Scotland, to bring back England to her allegiance. And though the Pilgrimage of Grace was within a fortnight extinguished in blood, the North rose again under Roger

Aske, on October 14, and for some months the issue was doubtful.

At the midnight Mass in St. Peter's, at Christmas 1536, three days after Pole had become Cardinal, the Holy Father solemnly blessed a cap and sword laid upon the High Altar, destined to be worn in defence of Holy Church by James of Scotland.*

Meantime the " visitations " continued, conducted by the two men whom a bigoted Protestant historian † styles " rash and

---

* The beautiful explanation given by Cardinal Pole, at their own request, of these symbolic gifts, to Philip and Mary, on April 28, 1555, cannot be passed over. " These gifts [are] blessed by the Vicar of Christ on earth on the night of the birth of Christ . . . to remind those who obtain . . . the sword . . . of justice, that if they wish to exercise it rightly they must first comprehend that they derive it from Christ Himself, with whom justice is twin-born. . . . The true use of the sword is shewn by the cap, decorated with pearls, representing a . . . dove . . . They who, together with the sword, receive the cap, are clearly taught that the power of the sword is not to be used by them according to their own arbitrament, but according to that of Him . . . who is Head and Lord of all ; this Head being the Holy Spirit, of which the purity of the pearls, and semblance of the dove, are symbols. . . . This is the true use of the sword. . . This is the signification of the cap." (" Venetian Calendar," vol. vi. 66.)

† Froude, " History," vol. iii., p. 98.

blameable ; " and who were in reality intolerable, sacrilegious scoundrels, whose very servants made rich apparel out of the stolen mass vestments in which they paraded the King's highway.* Everywhere was open pillage and robbery which could no longer be cloaked under the convenient name of " reform."

Into this terrible state of things it was the new Legate's duty to inquire. As it was perfectly certain that his head would not be safe for an instant should Henry hear of his landing, he was advised to remain on the Continent, and use every endeavour to promote a solid peace between the Emperor and the King of France, in view of the Catholic Alliance which seemed the only hope of saving England. It may be said here that the bitter political jealousy between the two rival monarchs was so great that all thought of touching Henry through them had to be abandoned, to their everlasting dishonour.

The Legate was also bidden to inform all the Princes through whose domains he passed of the Holy Father's intention to summon a General Council, and to beg their co-

* Rolls House M.S. Miscell., Ser. i., p. 402.

operation. If he found it impossible to visit officially the French court, Ghiberti, who was appointed his companion, was commissioned to do it for him.

Credentials were given him to the English nation, who were bidden to reverence and assist him ; to James of Scotland, who was exhorted to support him ; to the French King ; and to Mary, Dowager-Queen of Hungary, sister to the Emperor, and Regent of the Low Countries.

Pole, in a letter to the Pope, declares that he fears that Henry, in order to escape danger, and to put them off their guard, would profess compliance with the wishes of his Catholic subjects ; and then take a terrible vengeance upon them—which was exactly what did happen a few months later. Lest the nation should be terrorised he begs for active encouragement for the persecuted, and the opening, in Rome, of a fund for their relief.*

He considered the contract between the King and the nation void, by the breach of faith of the former, and the renouncing of that supremacy which for 900 years both sovereign and nation had professed ; for

* Ep. R. Poli, pars. 2a, p. 274.

which Fisher and More had gladly died, and for which he himself was an exile. Parliament, he added, was merely a tool in the King's hands.*

As he started on his perilous journey (February, 1537), he received a letter signed by all the members of the King's Council, repudiating *De Unitate Ecclesiæ ;* and stating that if he was not already a Cardinal they would willingly confer with him in Flanders, unofficially. To this Pole replied that he could not have written otherwise, and that as to the language complained of, only one copy had been sent, and that to the King, so no great harm had been done.† The French ambassador in Venice wrote to him to say he had sent a letter to the Lord High Steward of France, telling him what an illustrious visitor he might soon expect to receive.

Priuli, whom Pole called his *Achates,* and Beccadelli accompanied the Legate, as well as Ghiberti, and a small retinue. They started in Lent, and the health of the new Cardinal, far from robust, suffered greatly from fasting, though at first he refused to yield to his friends' remonstrances, and

* *De Unitate Ecclesiæ,* lib. i.
† Apol. ad Angl. Parl. Ep. R. Poli., pars. i., p. 179.

make any change in his diet. Later on he did so, on the strong representation of Contarini and Ghiberti; and writing to the former, he says that he feels better, and that his reason for refusing was the fear of setting a bad example. He begs Contarini, too, to remind the Pope to pray for him, for he is "much invigorated" thereby.[*]

At his farewell interview with the Holy Father he had asked but one thing—that he would remember him in his prayers.

From Piacenza, in the same delightful letter to Contarini, he explains that all his suite had gone out to explore the city, but his "golden shackles" kept him chained in his apartments; as a Papal Legate could scarely go about sight-seeing! Instead, he was writing to his friend, and realising what a solemn and awful thing he had undertaken.

At Lyons news came to him of the crushing of Roger Aske's rising by the blackest treachery on Henry's part. Things could scarcely be worse in England than they were now. "Henry VIII.," says an able non-Catholic writer,[†] "was a despot who

[*] "Venetian Calendar," v., p. 56.

[†] Gairdner, "History of the English Church in the Sixteenth Century," p. 187.

succeeded as few despots have done, in oppressing and slaughtering his subjects to gratify his own self-will; without interference either from powers at home, or from abroad."

At Paris the first check awaited Cardinal Pole. He was almost within reach of the terrible claws which the royal wild-beast stretched across the sea. The clergy and populace came out to meet him with every demonstration of honour, but the King was conspicuous by his absence; and later in the day sent a private letter to the Legate, begging him not to demand an audience—which to his grief he must refuse—but to leave Paris next day, and France as soon as possible. He had been warned, he said, " by an enemy of the Cardinal," to whom he could not " for his Kingdom's sake," refuse to listen. His personal feelings were very different, and the whole affair caused him deep sorrow. Henry, in defiance of all national law and courtesy, had actually requested Francis to deliver Pole into his hands as a traitor, and to send him in chains, a prisoner, to England!

Pole's gentle spirit was roused. In a letter to the Pope he says such conduct is

an outrage on all the laws which govern
Christian Kings ; and had he been sent on
a mission to a robber chieftain he could
scarcely imagine that the like would happen.
Francis, however, saw Ghiberti, and paid
every exterior mark of reverence and respect to the Legate.   More he could not afford
to risk.   The Legate proceeded to the Low
Countries, but was stopped at Cambray by
order of the Queen-Regent.   Pole gives a
graphic account of the event in a letter to
the Cardinal-Archbishop of Liège ; * and
in one to the Pope a few weeks later.†   The
messenger whom he sent to the Regent's
court was stopped at Valenciennes, and after
much delay, in response to his letter to the
Cardinal-Prince of Liège, a message came
to him from that prelate urging him to
come at once to Liège in disguise.   The
reason for this was soon apparent.   Henry
had been at work again.   The Archdeacon
of Cambray went to the Regent and brought
back a courteous message that she wished
personally to do the Legate every honour,
but in the present terribly strained political
situation she dared not give him audience,

* Ep. R. Poli, ii., p. 41.   April 27, 1537.
† *Ibid.*, p. 46.   May 15, 1537.

and thereby declare herself the open enemy of England. For this reason, and because she could not be officially aware of his presence, the Queen begged him to leave the Netherlands at once, and promised to conduct him to Liège with an armed escort if he would promise to do so. Henry's messenger, it seems, had just arrived at Brussels, warning the Regent against the Legate, and again begging that he might be betrayed and kidnapped, as a traitor.

After weighing the reasons for and against his immediate return to Rome, Pole goes on to say that he wishes to remain at his post, though the cause of England seems hopeless ; and mentions the price of £100,000, set by Henry on his head, adding that he had no fear ; though if he had, the example of Ghiberti would dispel it. The letter ends with these prophetic words : " If . . . the present generation transmit their opinions to their children, England will be for ever lost to the Church."

He spent a month at Cambray, where the air was rife with plots for his assassination, and messengers passed continually between the Queen-Regent, the Bishop of Cambray, and the Archbishop of Liège. The position was most awkward and uncomfortable; the town swarmed with freebooters and soldiers. Pole himself did not hold his life worthy of a day's purchase. But he saw clearly, as his official dispatches shew, that in all the seething tumult and smouldering discontent in England a moment might come for sudden action; and that it would be necessary for him to be on the spot. In a letter to Contarini he says he is far more conspicuous than he has any wish to be; and that a whole regiment of soldiers could change their quarters with greater privacy than he.

At the beginning of June he reached Liège. "They take him there," writes a spy of Cromwell's, "for a young god." * He wrote to the Pope, telling him that a journey of two days had taken forty— alluding to his detention at Cambray; and to Contarini to ask for money, pointing out pathetically that he is as economical as he can be—Ghiberti is treasurer and Priuli will bear him out that nothing is wasted; but that the expenses are very great, and they depend entirely upon the Pope's

* " Letters and Papers of Henry VIII.," xi. (ii.) p. 26. June 3, 1537.

generosity. He mentions a plot for his assassination by one of Henry's emissaries which was very nearly successful.* On the same day, June 10, he wrote to the Sacred College, begging for a letter of thanks to be sent to the Cardinal of Liège, on account of his great kindness and hospitality.

A few days later Henry sent an embassy to the Emperor, (in whose domains Pole was now living), offering him 500,000 golden crowns and 4,000 soldiers to fight against France, as the price of the Cardinal-legate, whom he desired to be delivered up alive, as a subject already attainted of treason!

Meantime, at Liège, enjoying the princely hospitality of the Cardinal-Prince, the little band spent three peaceful months, living almost as religious. They remained in their rooms, reciting the Divine office in private until Mass at 9. Dinner followed about 11; during which the Bishop of Verona read aloud from the works of St. Bernard. After dinner Ghiberti again read aloud some theological work, and then all talked for an hour or two. Vespers and

* " Venetian Calendar," v., p. 64.

Compline, which were said in public, followed
a rest of an hour and a half ; and then the
Legate expounded the Epistles of St. Paul
with " wonderful reverence, humility and
judgment," and the conference was followed
by supper. Then, in the sweet summer
evenings, they went for a walk in the fields
or country lanes ; and sometimes for a row
on the river.

" *Certe Deus nobis haec otia fecit ;* " said
Pole continually to Priuli, never failing,
says the latter, to add : " Why is not
Contarini here to enjoy it with us ? " The
little household was an oasis of prayer and
peace in a wilderness of hatred and war.

Nothing could be definitely effected for
England, however ; and on June 30, the
Pope, most anxious for Cardinal Pole's
presence in Rome, recalled him ; " as there
are at this difficult time many things on
which the [Holy Father] needs his advice." *

Before he left, the Regent received
Ghiberti very graciously, and sent many
messages to the Legate. But his best friend
had been the Cardinal Archbishop. With
exquisite delicacy he had insisted upon
cancelling a note for 1,500 crowns which

* Baronius, xxxii., p. 455.

Pole had given while awaiting supplies from the Papal exchequer, and added to this a gift of 2,000 crowns " as a token of his love ; " and before his guest's departure he spent three days in planning out a route by which Pole would be safe in travelling, and in friendly country.

Pole was still hopeful of a third rising in England, and was loth to leave his post of danger. "Of indignity," he said to Contarini,* who had expressed a doubt on the subject, " there is no fear, as nothing can be more dangerous than to dare to remain in such perilous places where least of all the enemy of the cause would wish them to be." †
On the eve of his departure he wrote to the Holy Father, saying that he is "always of the same opinion," but submitting entirely to the Pope's judgment. On August 22, 1537, the Legate left Liège, "riding solemnly through the city, giving his benediction to the people, with a cross borne before him, and other ceremonies. He was accompanied by the Cardinal of Liège, the Bishop of Verona, and the Nounce du Pappe.‡ "

* In a letter dated Liège, July 21, 1537.
† " Venetian Calendar," v. p. 66.
‡ Papal Nuncio. " Venetian Calendar," *ibid*.

After a difficult and perilous journey by way of Germany they reached Italy, where, just before arriving at Trent, Pole received a letter from Contarini, dated August 12, to say that the Pope permitted him to use his own discretion as to whether he returned or not. With gentle irony he remarked that perhaps it was well he had not received the mandate before leaving Liège ; and added that now his sacrifice would seem to be unnecessary. Priuli's friendship and devotion greatly consoled him at this time. " He is never far from me," he writes to Contarini, from Bovolona, Ghiberti's villa near Ostia.

He reached Rome at the beginning of October, 1537, and on the 19th gave a full account of his proceedings in Consistory,* laying down his legateship and returning to the quiet studious life which he loved better than any other. On November 3, he wrote a long and grateful letter to the Cardinal of Liège.†

His mission, from a human standpoint, had been almost completely a failure.

* " Letters and Papers of Henry VIII.," xii. (ii.) 949.
† Ep. R. Poli, ii., 92.

Sadolet, who wrote to console him, reminded him that in dealing with one absolutely devoid of morals or conscience, like Henry, who at the same time held the reins of power, failure was a foregone conclusion.

But neither failure nor success meant anything to Reginald Pole, whose soul was consumed with two passions—zeal for the Church, and love of his country ; and for their sake he was destined to accomplish greater things than these.

CHAPTER V

THE SECOND LEGATION

1538–1541

POPE PAUL III., in pursuance of his policy of peace, had prevailed upon the Emperor Charles and Francis I. to meet him at Nice, during the early summer of 1538. The outcome of the conference was a ten years' truce from June, 1538, and a promise from both monarchs to hold no further communication with Henry VIII., but to assist England to the utmost of their power to recover her lost faith. The Holy Father had insisted on Cardinal Pole's presence at the meeting—his unique position giving great weight to his advice—and the Emperor was most anxious to meet the man who had been the champion of Katherine of Aragon, whose nephew he was. Beccadelli tells us how on Charles' first visit to the Pope he specially inquired for the Cardinal, and received him " with the cordiality of a brother."*

Out of this meeting arose his second Legateship. Three years previously Henry had been solemnly excommunicated, but owing to the lack of unity among the powers, the sentence had never been published. Now that Charles and Francis were at peace, and every one was growing weary of Henry's increasing blasphemy and impiety, it was felt that a further step might be taken. On his return to Rome, December 17, 1538, the Pope renewed the bull of excommunication of August 30, 1535, by which Henry was deprived of his kingdom ; his subjects absolved from their allegiance ; and all Catholic princes exhorted to combine against him as an enemy of God and man. The immediate cause of the renewal was the outrageous sacrilege committed by Henry upon the shrine of St. Thomas of Canterbury, whose bones he burnt and scattered to the winds ; and whose tomb he had stripped of several cart-loads of gold and jewels—a crime reported in Consistory on October 25, 1538. All the other great shrines had already been

* Beccadelli. " Life of Cardinal Pole," p. 52. (Edn. 1766.)

desecrated and robbed ; this was the last—
and the greatest.

Pole was spending a few weeks at Priuli's
house at Trevilla, on his way back from
Nice, when the news reached him. Contarini was staying near, and the three
friends spent some happy days together ;
" St. Augustine and St. Basil," says Pole,
" being always of the company." It was
evidently here, though the fact seems to be
overlooked by his biographers, that Pole
made his retreat before receiving holy orders.
On December 12, 1538, Cromwell received
a despatch from a friend,* saying that
Pole had received the four minor orders from
Contarini on November 21, and the sub-
diaconate next day ; " and shortly intends
to proceed further." This the writer has
learnt in a letter from " Myhel Frognorton "
Pole's trusty servant. " They cannot,"
he adds, " have heard of the prisoners and
offenders in the Tower."

This piece of information is extremely
interesting, especially as it seems to be the
only reference in the State Papers or even
the Venetian Calendars, as to the reception

* " Letters and Papers of Henry VIII.," xiii.; (ii.),
1034.

of holy orders by the Cardinal; a matter which is passed over entirely by his biographers. Pole was, as a matter of fact, still ignorant of the fate of his hapless family, but when the news of the desecration of the shrine and the impending bull reached him he hastened to Rome, where the Pope urgently required his presence. Paul III. was well aware that without the co-operation of the Emperor and King Francis, the bull would have no effect upon Henry, and he intended to send Pole, who was eminently fitted for so delicate a mission, to Charles at Toledo, and thence to Francis at Paris, to remind both monarchs of the undertaking they had given, and to require them to carry it out.

On December 20, 1538, the day on which David Beaton, Bishop of St. Andrews, was raised to the Cardinalate as special adviser to King James of Scotland,* Cardinal Pole received his final instructions.† He was to point out to the Emperor the urgent need of an active alliance with France to bring Henry to his senses, in which he would be backed up warmly by James V. and his

---

* " Letters and Papers of Henry VIII.," xiii.; ii. p. 465.   † *Ibid.*, 1110.

new Cardinal; and that he should no longer suffer Henry " to rage with impunity against God and the saints hitherto worshipped by him and all the realm." Commerce with England was to be prohibited— a blow Henry could not fail to feel. As regards the Emperor's expedition against the Turks, the crusade against Henry being far more important, it would be better for the Holy League * and the King of France to make a truce with the former, and turn their attention to England. He was to point out, too, that, in case of the Emperor's absence against the Turks, the Lutherans assisted by England might make a very successful expedition against his own dominions.

It required a diplomatist to undertake such a mission, but its success mainly depended upon the disposition of the Emperor. Pole made the mistake, common to all generous natures, of judging others by himself. With so glorious an opportunity before him for the triumph of Holy Church it was impossible for the Cardinal to believe that Charles should not seize it.

* The " Holy League " was signed at Rome, against the Turks, by the Pope, the Emperor and the Venetian Government, November 3, 1538.

This, however, was not the Emperor's intention. Both he and Francis were men who put their visible kingdoms a very long way before the visible Church. Proud and obstinate, the man who held the balance of the power of Europe in his hands was only to be swayed by self-interest; and Francis, weak and vacillating, but well-meaning, dared not act alone; or do anything which might offend the Emperor, or Henry, or both. Each, terrified of playing into the hands of the other, contented himself by marking time vigorously, and loudly proclaiming his loyalty to the Church, and his hatred of heresy. The result of a legation to such men was again a foregone conclusion.

Before leaving Rome, at the beginning of January, 1539, Pole wrote to Cardinal Beaton a most tender and touching letter of encouragement in what promised to be for him the path of martyrdom—as indeed it proved to be. After reminding him of the special privilege of the successors of the Apostles to shed their blood for Christ he refers to the scarlet Cardinals' robes " which are worn so that should any ask, as the prophet did: ' why is thy garment red ? ' the [wearers] may answer as Christ did: ' because it behoves us to answer by deeds, not by words.' "*

On the feast of the Epiphany he reached Bologna. In order to render his journey safer it had been agreed that he should travel as a layman with a very small retinue ; as Henry's assassins lay in wait everywhere. Four days later, at Piacenza, his faithful friend Ghiberti met him, and tried to soothe the overwhelming grief of the Cardinal on receiving, the same day, an express sent after him from Rome, bringing the news that his whole family had been committed to the Tower.

This was Henry's vengeance for the first legation. In August, 1538, the suspicions of the doomed men were first roused. " The kyng," said Geoffrey Pole, " to be revenged off Reynold, I fere, will kyll us all."† A few days later he was imprisoned and closely examined. It was endeavoured to prove that he had sent money and assistance to his brother in the Low Countries ; and a certain priest, Hugh Holland, his

* " Quod Christus fecit, quod nos factis potius, quam verbis respondere decet."

† " Letters and Papers of Henry VIII.," xiii., (ii.), p. 313.

messenger, was strictly questioned. Father Holland had certainly seen the Cardinal at Liège, and his account of the interview is pathetic. At the end the Cardinal said : " Commend me to the lady my mother by the same token that she and I, looking upon a wall together read this: ' *Spes mea in Deo est ;* ' and desire her blessing for me . . Commend me to the Lord* my brother, by this token : ' *in Dño. confido ;* ' and bid my brother Sir Geoffrey meddle little, and let all things alone."†

Such charges as could be proved against Lord Montague were that he had said : " Reynold should do good some day ; " and that he himself had " never loved the King from childhood." The charge actually brought against him, and his cousin Lord Exeter, was that of conspiring to place Reginald Pole on the throne of England ! That they had sent money to the Cardinal they did not attempt to deny.

In October, 1538, Geoffrey Pole, under fear of torture and death, revealed in his seven " appearances " enough evidence of sym-

---

* Montague.

† " Letters and Papers of Henry VIII.," xiii.; (ii.), p. 310.

pathy, letters, and money having been sent to his brother to make the case for his family hopeless. On November 4, Lord Montague and Lord Exeter* were committed to the Tower as traitors, and Margaret Pole, Countess of Salisbury, was placed under arrest about the same time. On November 14, Lord Southampton and the Bishop of Ely wrote to Cromwell† "yesterday . . . we travailed with the Lady of Salisbury all day . . . till almost night; but for all we could do she would confess nothing . . . To-day . . . we repaired to her again. But first, as instructed, we called her men-servants before us . . . we then entreated her with all sorts, sometimes with doulx and mild words ; now roughly and asperly, by traitoring her and her sons to the ninth degree, yet will she nothing utter . . . surely if it like your lordship we suppose that there hath not been seen or [harde of a] woman so manlique‡ in continuance and so precise in words that wonder is to be.

* Next in succession to the throne if Henry died childless, through his mother Katherine, daughter of Edward IV. He was Henry VIII.'s first cousin. Reginald Pole was his second cousin.

† "Letters and Papers of Henry VIII.," xiii., (ii.), 345.   ‡ Manly.

For . . . she behaveth herself so . . . and all thing [so] sincere, pure and up[right] on her part that we have conceyved and needs must deem and think the one of two things, that either her sons have not made her privy and participant . . . or else she is the most errant traitress that ever lived." Two days later Blessed Margaret Pole wrote to her eldest son in the Tower :* "Son Montague, I send you God's blessing and mine. The greatest gift I can send is to desire God's help for you, for which I perceive there is need. My advice, in the case you stand in, is to endeavour to serve your prince without disobeying God's commandments."

She was removed in custody to Cowdray and her house at Warblington searched by Cromwell's orders. Copies of papal bulls and private documents were discovered, sufficient in themselves to incriminate her household.

On December 3, 1538, Montague and Exeter went through the mockery of a trial, and on the 9th were beheaded on Tower Hill with as many others as Cromwell could implicate. Geoffrey Pole received

* "Letters and Papers of Henry VIII." xii., (ii.), 357.

a free pardon, and lived and died a broken-hearted man.

" Blessed be the God of England that worketh all, whose instrument you are ! " wrote Latimer to Cromwell on December 13.*

" I heard you say once after you had seen that furious invective of Cardinal Pole that you would make him to eat his own heart ; which you have now (I trow) brought to pass, for he must needs now . . . be as heartless as he is graceless."

Pole's tender heart was wrung. Writing to Contarini† he points out how Henry had begun with priests and rulers ; gone on to slaughter the nobility ; and was now wreaking his vengeance on women and children.‡ He went on to Carpentras, where Sadolet was impressed by his calmness and fortitude. In Pole's place, he wrote to a friend in Rome, he should have been crushed under the burden of such suffering. The Cardinal's wonderful detachment seems to have struck everybody who met him. His private sorrow was too sacred for utterance ;

* " Letters and Papers of Henry VIII.," xiii., ii., p. 443.

† Ep. R. Poli, pars. 2a, p. 197.

‡ Lord Exeter's son, a boy of sixteen, was then in the Tower.

the only grief he expressed was for the public calamity which had befallen England.

From Carpentras, with four attendants, Pole and Ghiberti went on to Barcelona, which they reached at the end of January, 1539, only to find that Henry had been beforehand with them again, and had written to the Emperor a letter* which is certainly characteristic. He had heard, he says, that Cardinal Pole is on his way to sow discord throughout the Empire, and knew his nature to be so ungrateful that no good could come of it. While shedding crocodile's tears he would shed, if he could, the venom of his viper nature. He was a traitor, and had conspired to destroy the whole royal family! He concludes by begging for Pole's extradition. To this effusion Charles replied that even if Pole was a traitor to himself he could not refuse to receive him if he came as Papal Legate, and Henry's request was impossible. But Pole soon saw that the Pope had been misinformed as to the Emperor's dispositions and that he had not the slightest intention

* " Letters and Papers of Henry VIII.," xiv. (i.), p. 108.

of allowing the censures to be published in his domains.

He received the Legate coldly, but with every ceremony due to his position; and informed him that the present time was "unseasonable" for carrying out the Pope's wishes; adding that the bull should not have been published in Rome if there was no certainty of its execution. And in spite of all the arguments Pole advanced, in answer to the Emperor's excuses, it was perfectly clear that nothing was to be hoped from Charles. The Legate pointed out that the Pope did not wish for war, but that he hoped that by an alliance between Charles and Francis commerce with England would be so affected that the nation would rise as one man and compel Henry to submit. The Nuncio, who was present, reminded the Emperor that he had previously agreed to this, and even more; * but Charles was decided. Pole, on leaving, said with great charity to the councillors that: "His Majesty had much more good will to assist the cause of England than he shewed in words;" and that when the reason for reserve was removed he

* "Letters and Papers of Henry VIII.," xiv. (i.) 236.

would no doubt show his "good religious mind."

The Cardinal-legate was now in a most difficult position. If the King of France returned the same negative answer as the Emperor, it would, as he says : " be a very great wound to Mother Church," and make " the enemies of Holy See more insolent than ever." On the other hand, if Francis agreed to publish the censures the truce between the two monarchs on whom the peace of Christendom depended would be broken, and there would be no remedy.

He left Barcelona at the beginning of March, and instead of going himself direct to the French court, sent a messenger, Vincenzo Parpaglia, Abbot of San Salute in Turin, to find out the King's wishes privately, and bring word to the Legate at Carpentras. On March 16, he wrote to the Constable of France explaining his action, and begging him to obtain for the abbot a good audience.* Spain was no longer safe for him. Wyatt, the English Ambassador, had openly proclaimed his intention of assassinating the Legate "so soon as he

* " Letters and Papers of Henry VIII.," xiv. (i.), 536.

should be proclaimed traitor." Pole looked
upon these threats as the "vapouring of an
idle and profligate young man;" but when
shortly after, the Act of Attainder was
passed against him, and Wyatt suddenly
disappeared, he attached more importance
to them. From a despatch in cipher of
Wyatt's* it is perfectly evident that had
not the Legate changed his route suddenly,
after leaving Toledo, he would have been
murdered by an emissary of the accredited
English ambassador; and the plot was
without doubt known to Henry VIII.

The "sweetness and humanity" of
Cardinal Sadolet comforted him greatly
at Carpentras. He writes of his host to
Contarini, saying that the latter need not
ask how he was received, for in this house
he feels as if he were in a safe port after a
storm. "I have learnt," he adds, "from
some years' experience of all kinds of causes
that none are more difficult to obtain than
those which pertain to God and religion;
though men daily pray: *Thy will be done.*"†

During this month of March, 1539, there

---

* Printed for the first time in "Letters and Papers
of Henry VIII.," xiv. (i.), 560.

† Ep. R. Poli. ii., 146.

occurs, amongst Cromwell's " Remembrances " "a Bill of Attainder to be drawn . . . for the Lady of Salisbury. Another to be drawn for the false traitor Reynolde Pole and his fellows."* This was Henry's revenge for the Emperor's refusal to yield up the Legate. On March 30, Palm Sunday, a sermon was preached by Tunstall before the King, bitterly denouncing the action of the Pope in " moving war against England," and " in getting Reynolde Pole to stir up other nations against England, whose treasons have been disclosed by his own brother."

Henry was very nervous at this time, for in spite of the Emperor's refusal, the outlook was very serious. Ireland had rebelled, and appealed to the Pope. He could by no means depend on the neutrality of James V. of Scotland. A large fleet was in preparation off the coast of Holland, where a number of English ships had been " arrested." He went himself to inspect the coast defences. His late queen, Jane Seymour, had died October 24, 1537, twelve days after the birth of her son,

* " Letters and Papers of Henry VIII.," xiv. (ii.), 655.

Prince Edward; and from the day of her death, Cromwell had been urging him to strengthen his hands by a Protestant marriage—which, however, was distasteful to Parliament. A "Protestant League" was one of Cromwell's favourite plans. His influence, however, was waning. His work had been done so thoroughly that Henry could gain little more from him. Nearly all the monasteries were confiscated to the tyrant, and the few which were left would fall immediately. In June one sweeping Act of Attainder was passed, including in its meshes living and dead; Lords Montague and Exeter, Margaret Pole, and her son Reginald, with many others; most of whom were executed at once.

That Henry recognised the Pope and the Legate as his chief dangers is abundantly shown by contemporary MSS. In a commission for musters* dated May 8, 1539, we have such words as these: "the realm . . . of which his Highness alone is King and Supreme Head, under God [has lately heard that], the cankered and venomous serpent, Paul, Bishop of Rome, by that arch-traitor Reygnold Pole, enemy to God's

* "Letters and Papers of Henry VIII.," xiv. (ii.)

word and his own natural country, had moved, excited and stirred divers great princes and potentates of Christendom not alonely to invade this realm of England with mortal war, but also by fire and sword to extermine and utterly to destroy the whole nation and generation of the Same." In another state paper * speaking of the English abbots, we read : " I think . . . our Mother Holy Church of Rome, hath not so great a jewel of her own darling Raynolde Poole," and later, " his crafty cardinality." " Could a man wish Poole greater wretchedness, which, the longer he lives, the greater his shame ? " In April, 1539, the Papal Ambassador at the French court wrote privately to the Legate at Carpentras, warning him that it was useless to hope for definite help from Francis, who would " do nothing without Charles."

To this disappointment was added the crushing blow of the Attainder. " As for myself," wrote Pole to Contarini, " I am compassed with such a variety of afflictions that I scarcely know how to extricate myself."† He was now, with Bembo and

* " Letters and Papers of Henry VIII.," xiv. (ii.) 613. † Ep. R. Poli, ii., 149.

Priuli, lodging in a monastery at Carpentras, leading much the same kind of life as at Liège. He tells Contarini that they have begun conferences on the Psalms ; and had that day meditated upon the one beginning " Save me, O God, because truth has left the children of men ; " adding very sadly : " whoever has much to do with them cannot doubt their treachery." In August, the Pope recalled him to Rome, where his presence was greatly needed, but through Contarini he obtained continued leave of absence, on account of his having so lately heard of the death or imprisonment of nearly all his relations.

" My mother," he says to his friend, " has been sentenced to death—that is, to Life Eternal."

On the death of Cardinal Campeggio, Legate in the late divorce, Pole was offered by the Pope the Bishopric of Salisbury. But he refused, saying with quiet humour that in the present state of things he might as well be Bishop of Antioch ! Sadolet wrote about this time to Cardinal Farnese, describing his friend's admirable behaviour during these sad months, and his " wisdom, modesty and religion," adding that it greatly redounded to the credit of Holy See for foreign countries to note that such men were placed at the helm.

Pole left Carpentras in October, 1539. Between Aix and Marseilles he visited the great shrine of St. Mary Magdalene at Ste. Beaume, to pray there for the conversion of Henry VIII. and for England. But he found no consolation there. Like the prophet of old, he seemed to hear a voice which said: "Why dost thou intercede for him whom I have cast off?" and he went on his way heavy-hearted. He passed a few weeks with the Bishop of Verona. The air was rife with the rumours of his assassination. Henry was even then doing his best to bring about the removal of the man he feared and hated by means of hired murderers, and his intended victim seemed to think it likely he would be successful. "Though safe at present, I never feel secure." Especially did he dread the return to Rome, where a plot was known to be laid. He was evidently still suffering severely from nervous and mental strain, and the thought of his heroic mother in prison must continually have haunted him.

He was annoyed on reaching Rome,

to find that *De Unitate* was on the point
of being published without his knowledge
or permission. He prefixed, however, to
the edition, an open letter to the Emperor,
as the most powerful Catholic sovereign
in Europe, explaining his reasons for having
written the book.*

Meanwhile in England, Henry's fourth
wife, the Protestant Princess Anne of
Cleves, landed in December, 1539, and was
regarded with much disfavour by that
monarch ; though in truth she was but a
necessary factor in Cromwell's pet scheme,
the alliance of Protestant Princes, which
eventually wrought his ruin.

About Christmas-time Cardinal Pole was
appointed by the Pope Governor of Viterbo,
the most important of the Papal provinces ;
situated in the heart of Italy ; Viterbo
itself being only twenty miles from Rome.
It was a mark of great confidence, and
Pole was sincerely grateful for the opportunity it afforded him of returning to
his quiet life of prayer and study. He
wrote to the Holy Father, thanking him
warmly.†

* Apologia ad Carolum Caesarem.
† " Venetian Calendar," v., 81.

On the Feast of the Epiphany, 1540, a formal alliance was contracted between Henry VIII. and Anne of Cleves; and from that moment Cromwell's downfall was sure; though Henry masked his intentions with hideous cunning, heaping him with titles and honours. The blow was sharp and sudden. On June 10, he was arrested at the council-board on a charge of treason. He dashed his cap on the ground in a passion of fury, but was stripped of his decorations and conveyed to the Tower. Following his own precedent for Blessed Margaret Pole a bill of attainder was passed against him, from which he was not heard in his own defence. As he lay in prison Parliament passed the Bill of Divorce between Henry and Anne on July 12, 1540—no reference being considered necessary, this time, to the Pope. Cromwell had been actually brought out of prison to give evidence in Henry's favour, but even this could not save him; nor the abject letters he wrote and which Henry read " with tears "—letters " written with the heavy heart and trembling hand of your Highness' most heavy and most miserable prisoner and poor slave, Thomas Cromwell. Most gracious Prince, I cry for mercy, mercy, mercy."[*] He died horribly on Tower Hill, July 28, 1540 ; and on the same day Henry, who was certainly an epicure in sensations, married Katharine Howard.

In the meantime Pole lived quietly at Viterbo, spending much time in prayer ; and making many friends in his pleasant surroundings. Here he founded a Literary Society, of which he was elected President, and in which were enrolled some of the greatest geniuses of the day. Even a few celebrated women were admitted as members, one of the most remarkable being Vittoria Colonna, Marchesa di Pescara, whose husband, a most gallant soldier, had, after winning the battle of Pavia, refused the crown of Naples. Shortly after her husband's death she left Viterbo to enter a convent at Orvieto, where on April 15, 1541, the Cardinal writes of her to a mutual friend as well and happy. At her death, a few years later, she left Pole a legacy of 10,000 crowns ; which he bestowed as a dowry upon her niece—an eminently characteristic act.

Two direct attempts upon Cardinal Pole's

* (Dugdale) Baronius, vol. ii., pp. 372-3.

life had now been made by Henry's hired assassins ; the ruffians being caught in both cases. In the first instance at Viterbo, they were tried and released by Pole ; in the second, at Capranica, he sent his would-be murderers—two of whom were Englishmen—to the galleys for a few days. When remonstrated with by his friends, who were terribly anxious as to his safety, he said that as the offence was solely against himself the punishment ought surely to be at his own discretion !

The men were nominally Lutherans, and, incredible as it may sound, upon his leniency towards them was based the absurd charge of heresy, actually brought against the Angelical Cardinal a few years later.

On May 28, 1541, at 7 A.M. Blessed Margaret Pole, the King's cousin, then seventy years old, was martyred on Tower Hill, after an imprisonment of two years.

When the letter containing the awful news reached Cardinal Pole, says Beccadelli, who gave it to him, he sat for a time in silence ; and then said quietly that he had thought himself blessed by God in having so noble and virtuous a mother ; but from henceforward he could call himself the son of a martyr. Henry, he added, had thus recompensed one, who after his own children was nearest to him in blood, for the care of his daughter's education, lasting many years ; and for all the care and affection the countess had lavished on the Princess Mary. Then, seeing Beccadelli's horror the Cardinal added with deep emotion, " Be of good cheer—we have one patron the more in heaven ! " On August 1 he wrote to the Cardinal Archbishop of Burgos in reply to a letter of condolence, that he was now the son of a martyr, "which is certainly grander than to be born of any royal race " : that his mother was the cousin of Henry VIII., "worthy of all honour from piety and age : and such death was no ignominy, since to suffer as Christ, the apostles, virgins and martyrs suffered is no disgrace : and that the less consolation can be hoped from nature, the more can be expected from God."*

To Cardinal Marcello, afterwards Pope, he wrote at the same time a touching letter, saying that if the shedding of his own blood was necessary to fill up the measure of

* " Venetian Calendar," v., 108.

Blessed Margaret of Salisbury.

Henry's iniquity, and bring about his conversion, he (Pole) "desires nothing more than that the deed be done forthwith." On the Feast of the Assumption he wrote to thank Vittoria Colonna for the prayers of her convent, by which he had been greatly sustained.

His heroic fortitude and detachment made a vivid impression on all who knew him. All his natural sorrow was drowned in supernatural joy. His mother was in Heaven, and he too was ready to follow, by the same road of tears and blood.

His firmness in the matter of the King's divorce, says an old chronicler,* was the cause of "the death of the virtuous lady the countes of Salysbery his mother . . . Surely thys cruelty was great, but that whyche exceeded all the rest : thys olde ladye being at least lx and x yeares of age, cosin to the king, and beyng (as is saied) most innocent and giltles, was without judgement or processe of lawe, drawen by

* John Elder. "A breve overture . . . of the legacion of the moste reverende father in God, lorde cardinall Poole, from the Sea Apostolyke of Rome." *circa* 1555. Republished by Camden Society, 1850.

the hore heres * to the blocke, not knowyng
any cause why, to dye."

But even yet the King's vengeance was
unsatisfied.

Hoar hairs.

CHAPTER VI

THE GENERAL COUNCIL

1542–1547

IN 1542 the long talked-of Council was at last called. The position was a critical one. Reforms, both internal and external, were terribly needed. Luther's heresy had overrun Germany, and called for definite action; while England, as the natural consequence of Henry VIII.'s schism was fast falling under the same dangerous influence. On the other hand, the discipline of the Church needed strong enforcement, especially in individual cases, and it was felt that a General Council could no longer safely be delayed.

In January, 1542, a Diet of the Empire was held at Spires, at which the Papal Legate moved the holding of such a council at Trent in the following November ;* and

* State Papers, 34 Henry VIII., ix., 155.

this was agreed to, in spite of strong opposition from the Protestant faction. Trent, situated in neutral territory, in Northern Italy, not too far from France or Germany, was admirably suited for the purpose, being healthy, and cool in summer, with a delightful climate.

The Pope sent three Legates, Cardinals Parisius, Morone, and Pole. They were charged to notify the Council publicly to all; not to enter into argument with heretics in the presence of the Council, or to permit such arguments; and not to open the proceedings until the proper number of representatives had arrived.

It was a position of grave responsibility, requiring infinite tact. Charles and Francis were now at war; and though the opening of the Council was announced for November 1, All Saints' Day, no French bishops appeared at all, and only a few Italian and Spanish prelates.

The Pope refused to allow the Council to be opened, and to the keen disappointment of Cardinal Pole, recalled the Legates early in 1543. He was still mourning the loss of his dear friend Contarini, who, on August 4,

1542,* had died while on his way to the
Emperor, as Papal Legate, to attempt to
make peace between Charles and Francis;
but his personal sorrow was whelmed in
the intense grief which he felt at the apparent failure of the Council. He retired to
his domain of Viterbo; and there, a few
months later, learnt of the death of another
close friend, Bishop Ghiberti of Verona.
This prelate had been one of the first to
recognise and appreciate Pole's extraordinary
gifts of mind and character, nearly twenty
years before, and had sympathised with
and encouraged him in all his troubles. A
man of charming personality, and eminent
sanctity, Ghiberti was known throughout
Europe as a brilliant scholar, and his death
was a terrible blow to Pole, who, within a
few months, had lost two of his best friends.

The next three years passed quietly at
Viterbo; while in England, Henry, having
by now squandered the revenues and
possessions of the religious houses, proceeded to sequestrate and appropriate the
collegiate churches, chantries, guilds, and
even hospitals; so that nothing was now
left untouched except the bishoprics. In

* " Spanish Calendar," **v**i., (ii.) p. 50.

1545, peace having been temporarily arranged between France and the Empire, the Council of Trent was again summoned. Pole, now Cardinal-Deacon of St. Mary in Cosmedin, was again chosen as Legate, together with Cardinal del Monte, Bishop of Palestrina, and the future Pope Marcellus II., Cardinal-priest di Santa Croce-in-Gerusalemme. Three other ecclesiastics were sent with them by the Pope, and all arrived at Trent in the beginning of March, except Pole, who appeared a month later. This was on account of a simple, but ingenious device by Henry VIII. to assassinate him, which made it necessary for him to travel incognito and by a circuitous route. The Bishop of Trent had written to warn him that two Italian ruffians, a certain Count Bonifacio, and the notorious Ludovico dell' Armi, had been hired to murder him on the road. A most interesting account of the exploits of the latter villain is given by the Venetian Government at this time to their secretary in England. He was the head of a band of thirteen hired assassins, maintained by Henry VIII. in Italian and Venetian territory,* earning

* *See* " Venetian Calendar," v., pp. 334–353.

(the word is significant) a monthly pension of 200 crowns in time of peace, and 50 in time of war. At this very time he was outlawed for brawling and murder in Venice, and on repeating the crime at Treviso, he was sentenced to death in August, 1545. He escaped; was recaptured, and beheaded on the Piazzetta di San Marco, at Venice, between the two great columns, a couple of years later. The Venetian Government, anxious not to offend Henry, requested their secretary to represent these facts to the King—the English ambassador having told them that they would " greatly displease his Majesty," to which the Council of Ten replied with dignity that " the King's friendship could not suffer hurt from the misdemeanours of such scoundrels."* Such were the tools which the King's conscience now allowed him to employ.

Pole, however, thanks to the warning, escaped unhurt, and came by way of Mantua, employing his enforced leisure in writing his celebrated " Treatise on General Councils,"† in which he shows that all have

* " Venetian Calendar," v., 348.

† The work was not published till 1562, some years

" proceeded on the plan of that held in Jerusalem." He insists particularly on the spirit of penance, which should animate all orders, and the reform especially needed amongst the clergy, adding that if these conditions were fulfilled the future Council might be compared not only to that of Nice, but to that first great Council held by the Apostles.

The Emperor had sent his ambassador, Mendoza, to excuse his attendance under the plea of illness. The King of France wrote a long letter to say that the French bishops were on their way. On December 13, 1545,* the legates, with the bishop, made their public entry into Trent, and formally opened the Council. Having vested in full pontificals at the Church of the Holy Trinity, together with the other ecclesiastics, also fully vested, they sang the *Veni Creator* before forming in procession. The religious orders went first, next the collegiate chapters and the secular clergy ; after whom came the bishops, the

after Pole's own death and that of Pope Paul IV., to whom, by a curious irony of circumstance, it was dedicated.

* *See* Pallavicini " Histoire du Concile de Trente," livre v., p. 1082.

legates walking at the end, before the ambassadors of the King of the Romans. They passed through the town to the Cathedral of St. Vigilius, and there the chief legate sang pontifical High Mass, giving a plenary indulgence to all those present, and enjoining them to pray for the peace of the Church and the nations. An eloquent Latin sermon was preached by a Franciscan friar, the Bishop of Bitonto ; after which certain prayers were recited, and the legate blessed the whole assembly thrice. The Litany of the Saints was then sung, and Cardinal del Monte, the President, asked if all were agreed that the Council was opened, to which all replied, *Placet*. He then asked them, whether, in view of the holy season of Christmas now close at hand, they would agree to fix the first session for January 7— the day after the Feast of the Kings. And all replied, *Placet*. After formal record had been made of questions and replies, a solemn *Te Deum* was sung ; the legates unvested, and wearing their cardinals' robes, preceded by the great silver cross at the head of the long procession of bishops and priests, proceeded to their lodging.

At this solemnity there were present

besides the three legates and the Cardinal-Bishop of Trent, four archbishops, twenty bishops, the generals of five religious orders, the auditor of the Rota, and the imperial ambassadors.

Great rejoicings took place in Rome, where Pope Paul III. published a Bull of Jubilee. During the suspension of the sessions at Christmas, the legates sent to ask his guidance as to the direction of the Council, and the manner of discussing the various questions. On January 7, 1546, after several informal meetings the first session was held,* the Bishop of Castella-mare singing High Mass, and the Bishop of St. Mark's preaching; after which the secretary read aloud, in the name of the legates, an exhortation written by Pole, chiefly on the necessity of preparing for the descent among them of the Holy Ghost by true contrition, compunction, and an exemplary life. The officiating bishop then read aloud the Papal constitutions and decrees, and the work of the Council was begun, it being henceforth declared sacred and œcumenical. At the fifth session, on June 17, two decrees were passed concerning Faith

* Histoire du Concile de Trente," livre vi., p. 44.

(in which heresies were condemned), and concerning Original Sin, in which great prominence was given to the Doctrine of the Immaculate Conception. Cardinal Pole was engaged in a discussion as to the *Filioque* clause, which he said was not used before the first Council of Ephesus, and quoted St. Thomas Aquinas to prove that that Council declared that: " the third person of the Trinity proceeds from the Father and the Son "; and that the creed was first read with this addition at the first Council of Toledo, probably prior to that of Chalcedon. He wrote from memory, without books of reference.

A few days afterwards he fell ill, and was obliged to go to Trevilla, Priuli's villa between Padua and Venice, the climate of which always suited him. His illness appears to have been acute rheumatic gout, to which he was a continual martyr. He wrote to the legates to say that his left arm and shoulder were almost useless, and his eye gave him ceaseless pain. He was, however, better, he said, but two Paduan physicians had told him that he must take care lest he should have a " stroke of palsy; " and had advised his consulting

Frascatorio, the great Veronese doctor.* Later on he wrote to say that the doctors had warned him, as he was growing worse, that if he returned to Trent he would probably be lame for life ; which, he quaintly adds : " can serve no purpose." In order that there should be no doubt at all about the question, he had sent, he says, his former messenger, Parpaglia, to Rome, in order to ascertain the will of the Holy Father as to his returning to Trent, or remaining where he was.† It is necessary to dwell on this fact ; as Protestant historians— and at the time his personal enemies—have not hesitated to affirm that he left the Council because he was not in agreement with it. One of the principal proofs of his sympathy is the fact that whenever possible he induced absentee members to return to the Council at once.

The Pope was now considering the advisability of transferring the Council to Bologna, a town in Papal territory. It was rumoured that plague had broken out at Trent, and this created somewhat of a panic even among the ecclesiastics. The district

* Ep. R. Poli, 4a., p. 189.
† Ibid., 4a., p. 193.

swarmed, too, with Lutheran troops ; and the Emperor, who considered himself politically slighted, was behaving in a domineering and disagreeable manner. However, in July 1546, the French delegates, who had been withdrawn, were sent back ; and the Pope dispatched to Trent two of the first companions of St. Ignatius, Fathers Laines and Salmeron, S.J. On July 17 the decree concerning Justification began to be discussed. It was this particular discussion which Pole's enemies had said he was anxious to escape ; some going so far as to accuse him indirectly of leanings towards Lutheranism on this question. In a dignified letter the cardinal explains his attitude on the subject ; pointing out that St. Paul and St. James, the respective exponents of justification by faith and by works, are not to be privately interpreted, put in opposition to each other, or understood singly ; but solely in the light and by the teaching of the Church which combines and unites their doctrine ; an advantage only to be gained by submission to her authority, and reliance on that foundation which is the base of truth.

If his enemies needed a further refutation

of their ridiculous charge they found it in the fact that the Council so missed the wisdom of the Angelical Cardinal in their deliberations that they sent a copy of their resolutions on the question of Justification to Pole, at Padua, for his criticism and approval. He was too ill to express an opinion at the time, but wrote a line of gratitude and acknowledgment ; and four days later sent Priuli to Trent, to express his views on the subject ; with which the Council declared itself satisfied.

A few weeks before, on May 29, 1546, Cardinal Beaton (whose unflinching courage and enthusiasm had caused Henry VIII. much uneasiness, as to the attitude of Scotland in his regard) was assassinated in the Castle of St. Andrews by the instigation and with the unfeigned approval of that monarch. The significance of this crime was by no means lost upon Cardinal Pole, who had foreseen it from the first.

On October 4 we have a charming letter from him to the Marchesa di Pescara, in the Orvieto Convent ; expressing the pleasure it gave him to receive a visit from her son Lelio (a boy of sixteen), and describing, with a good deal of quiet humour, how the boy had scolded him for his want of return for all his mother's affection. He, Pole continues, said nothing, intending Lelio to draw his own conclusion ; but he explains to his adopted mother that in some friendships one has to be content, like him who bade the poor to a feast, to give, but not to receive, and " such love is not the least blessed." He speaks, too, of " Divine . . . Charity which, though not reciprocated by its object, does not, however, weary of continuing its goodness." Describing his happiness in Cardinal Bembo's palace, at Padua, where he was then a guest, he says he feels as if it were his father's house, and that here were " two things in which I have always greatly delighted, a study, and a garden ; both of which I have found in such perfection here that to my taste I should be unable to find more beautiful anywhere."* The death of Cardinal Bembo, one of his oldest and dearest friends, a few months later,† was a blow which he felt with the whole of his gentle, affectionate nature. But while he was mourning his loss, the Council of Trent, which had again

* " Venetian Calendar," v., 172.
† January 15, 1547.

met on January 13, to discuss the question of Justification and good works, requested him to draw up the decree on this doctrine; and this he did in his own handwriting. After this there can be little doubt in what light the Church regarded him.

And then a great event happened. On January 28, 1547, Henry VIII., tyrant, schismatic, heretic—whose last act was to "drink a great goblet of wine"; whose last awful words were: "Lost, lost, all lost!"—was called to appear before the Judgment Seat of God.

CHAPTER VII

THE CONCLAVE

1547–1553

EDWARD VI., a little boy not ten years old, was brought from Hertford to London, upon the death of his father, by his mother's brother, the Earl of Hertford, who, immediately after Henry VIII.'s funeral, took the title of Duke of Somerset, and became Lord Protector of the realm. To this man, a peculiarly bigoted Protestant, were due not only the continued exile of Cardinal Pole, but the lapse into hopeless heresy into which the country now fell. One of his first acts was to issue, in the King's name, a general pardon, from which, however, four names were excluded, one being that of Reginald Pole.

The year 1547 was a year of deaths. Upon that of Henry VIII. Cardinal Pole wrote with equal generosity and charity: " In his words and most unjustifiable actions he never failed to allege the motive of conscience and religion."*

No one else attempted to say more, or even as much; † and the terrible man whose very death no one had dared to proclaim for three days after it had taken place, so greatly was he dreaded, went to his account amid the unspeakable, if unspoken, relief of his entire kingdom. Pole wrote to Paul III. advising him of the great opportunity which seemed to be presented now in England, and of the certainty that the Emperor would help in the establishment of peace and true religion ; and saying that from his personal knowledge he felt sure that the most acceptable legate for this mission would be the Cardinal of Trent, who " never thinks he has done anything till he has brought it to a conclusion."‡ He wrote, too, to the Privy Council of England, freely forgiving the injuries done to his family, saying that the Holy Father proposed sending him as legate to his

* Ep. R. Poli, 1a., p. 145.

† Sir Walter Raleigh wrote, later : " If all the examples of a merciless Prince were lost, they could be found in him."

‡ Ep. R. Poli, 4a, pp. 38, 39.   The Pope, however, preferred Cardinal Pole.

country and begging them to receive him, in the Pope's name.* This letter, however, was refused, not being read, or even opened by the Council. Feeling was evidently strong against him. Not losing heart, Pole sent two of his household to England to ascertain the state of affairs. They spent some time on the way thither at the Emperor's court, where they consulted Father Soto, his Dominican confessor, as to what they should do—the influence of Charles being at this time great in England. This was in April 1547. At the same time Pole wrote a Treatise to the young King, which he intended to prefix to a new edition of *De Unitate;* explaining the writer's attitude to Henry VIII., and the reasons which had compelled him to write that work. The tone of the letter was manly and dignified, and should have impressed Edward ; but it is more than probable he was never allowed to see it. England now, under Somerset's rule, was given up to Protestantism. The last gleanings of the shrines and holy places—the rich harvest reaped by Henry VIII.—were now gathered in ; and the doctrines of the German

* Ep. R. Poli, 4*a*, p. 42.

heretics*—especially those of Zuinglius—
were incorporated into the new forms of
worship. Edward VI. did not protest,
like his father, that he lived and died " as
good a Catholic as any " ; he gloried in his
Protestantism. The schism of Henry VIII.
had brought forth its poisonous inevitable
fruit—the heresy of his son.

On March 31 died Francis I., King of
France, who was succeeded by his son,
Henry II., perhaps as great a time-server
as his father. At the beginning of the same
month Cardinal Pole lost his great friend,
Vittoria Colonna, Marchesa di Pescara,
who passed away peacefully in the Convent
of Orvieto. From Rome, on March 5, Pole
writes a very tender letter of sympathy to
her son, for whom he had a warm affection.
The Marchesa seems to have been almost
the only woman, with the exception of his
mother, and Queen Mary, with whom
Pole was on terms of friendship, or with
whom he corresponded. After his mother's
martyrdom he had taken Vittoria Colonna,
as he told her, for a second mother, and he

* One of whom found no less than twelve different
meanings for the words of Institution and rejected
Baptism as " savouring of idolatry."

was in the habit of writing to her when he wanted prayers for any special intention, which she obtained for him in her convent. His letters to her are very beautiful. On March 9, 1547, the Council met once more at Trent ; when a decree concerning the reform of the clergy was passed, and then the Pope adjourned it to Bologna. Charles V. was excessively angry, and withdrew his representatives. As temporal rulers he always distrusted the Popes, and suspected Paul III. of some political design in removing the Council from neutral into Papal territory—a suspicion absolutely unjustified by facts.

Pole was kept at Rome by the Holy Father, who during the acute diplomatic crisis, felt the urgent necessity of his wisdom and tact, in dealing with the infuriated sovereign ; besides which, the affairs of the Council pressed heavily, and of these, no one understood the details like Pole. He was too honest and straightforward to become a great diplomatist—at any rate in those days—but the deep respect which even Charles felt for him, and his universal reputation for sanctity, as well as knowledge and wisdom, gave his advice great weight.

Much time was consumed over the negotiations with Mendoza, the Imperial ambassador, and at last Pole drew up his final pronouncement to the Emperor, in which he warned him that no heresies—nor even the Emperor himself—could overthrow the Catholic Church or impeach its authority, Jesus Christ having said that the gates of hell should not prevail against it.

He was so far successful that two Spanish delegates sat at Bologna on January 16, 1548 ; but Charles, whose pride was deeply hurt, and who was very angry at the delay of the Council—which was entirely caused by his own action—chose to draw up for the benefit of his subjects, a confession of faith, called the *Interim*, in July, 1548. It was to be in force until the General Council came to a decision upon the points in question. It was an unheard-of thing for a Catholic sovereign to do, and Charles was perfectly aware of the fact. Nevertheless, it was received at the Diet of Augsburg. It consisted of thirty-six articles, two at least of which (as to the marriage of priests, and communion in both kinds) were displeasing to Catholics

Cardinal Pole was desired to write against

it, which he did, from Viterbo, plainly setting
forth its evil tendency, and speaking the
truth quite fearlessly to Charles, who had
enough generosity in his character to appreciate his courage.

Meanwhile little was done at Bologna.
Both French and Imperial representatives
had been withdrawn, and only the Italian
ecclesiastics were present. Paul III., in
despair, decided to prorogue the Council
indefinitely ; and this was done on Good
Friday, 1549, to the intense grief of Pole,
who shed bitter tears at what seemed the
downfall of all his hopes for reformation
within and without. The Pope had declared
his intention of establishing a congregation
in Rome, to deal with matters of reform
and discipline, but that did not comfort
him.

Writing to a friend he speaks of the great
hopes he had had of the work of the Council,
but that in spite of the present cruel disappointment he trusted implicitly in God ;
" after the example of the disciples, who
hoped in Him against hope itself." He
points out, in describing his own feelings,
the analogy of the day : " I was no otherwise affected than if I saw my Saviour's

dead body before my eyes." He firmly hoped, however, through these sufferings, to see the resurrection: " So His mystic body, the Church . . . might rise again . . . the Holy City, the new Jerusalem."*

In June 1549, we find him spending the summer at Civitella, a beautiful place twenty miles from Rome, to which the Pope had given him leave to retire during the heats. He was staying in a castello belonging to the monks of St. Paul. He wrote to a friend that it was " a very convenient and opportune place for the season," and he hoped to pass the rest of the summer there.†

On June 4 the Protector Somerset wrote him an insolent letter,‡ from Greenwich, in answer to the Cardinal's of May 6 (of which we have no record in the State Papers). He hoped, he said, that Pole at last perceived the " errors and abuses of the Church of Rome " ; and urged him to take advantage of the King's " mercy," and return to England. He also sent him—evidently with perfect gravity—a copy of the " Book of Common Prayer " ! This was the " First

* Ep. R. Poli, 4a, pp. 65–68.
† " Venetian Calendar," v., 563.
‡ " Domestic Papers of Edward VI.," June 4, 1549.

Prayer book of Edward VI.," a far more
" Catholic " production than the second,
which was published in 1552, and is still used
in the Church of England, though with some
slight modifications in a Catholic direction.

On September 7 Pole replied * to this
effusion,† which he said he should rather
take to be the work of some ignorant secretary than that of a gentleman of Somerset's
undoubted birth and breeding. He wrote
to the Protector what is practically a
Treatise, in which with infinite patience
he once more described his dealings with
Henry VIII., and the utterly unjustifiable
anger with which that monarch received
his conscientious opinion about the Divorce
and Royal Supremacy. Yet, says the
Cardinal, the King, *after having read it*,
had said to Lord Montague, when walking
with him in " a privy garden " : " that
I had spoken the truth, nor could . . .
[he] . . . ever feel any anger against me,
as although the writing was very contrary
to his will, he nevertheless recognised in it
my love for him, and the sincerity with
which I had written it."

* " Venetian Calendar," v., 241–267.
† Somerset's letter.

The Cardinal declines the invitation sent by the Council to return and become one of their number, in spite of Somerset's information that through that enlightened body " the purity of the Word of God, and the doctrine of Christ [was] sent forth . . . and taught more purely now than ever it was before." He speaks most powerfully about the title " natural and supreme Lord," assumed by Edward, which he does not deny " may be true in one sense."

The Treatise is too long and deals with subjects too important to be paraphrased even in outline, but every word is of the deepest interest, and it amply repays careful study. In conclusion, Pole warns Somerset of the great and terrible dangers to which England is exposed—which the Protector will not see ; desiring " no other grace of omnipotent God than what is for [its] safety and for the Honour of his Divine Majesty, whom may it please to have under his merciful protection, you, and the whole kingdom."

The Cardinal wrote from Rome, where stirring events were about to take place, of which we have a most vivid—and very often a most amusing—picture in the letters to his government of Matteo Dandolo, the Venetian ambassador in the holy city. He seems to have been a delightful, but slightly irreverent person, with a keen sense of humour ; and was also evidently a man of considerable influence and importance.

On November 10, 1549, Pope Paul III. died, and his successor was not declared until February 7, 1550, after the longest conclave (then) on record. On the day of his death Pole—whose name was in the mouth of every one as the future Pope— became titular Abbot of Sta. Maria di Gavello, on the Polesine. Dandolo tells us* (though the epigram is necessarily spoilt in translation) : " his Right Reverend Lordship is styled Angelical rather than Anglican " (*porta piu presto nome di Angelico che di Anglico*), or, as another puts it : *non Anglus sed Angelicus.*

He had been the head of the late Pope's Council, and necessarily took a leading part in affairs when the Conclave was assembling, though not after it was, on November 30, " closed," *i.e.*, walled-up in the Vatican. He spent the long weeks almost entirely in his cell, writing a very important treatise

* " Venetian Calendar," v., 587.

on the duties of that Pontificate to which it was his daily prayer that he might not be called . . . if such were the will of God.

On December 5, Dandolo writes* : " Until after the eighteenth hour we remained [outside the Vatican] awaiting the announcement of [Pole's] election ; and then . . . people drew breath, for no one can imagine how very unpopular it is, as they consider that the whole of this court would have to lead a new life . . . but the minority wishes for it greatly." He was, as the Archbishop of Cornaro tersely puts it† : " A man of everlasting virtue ; and such, in the sixteenth century, were not always the most popular candidates for the Papacy."

The contemporary letters and documents in the State Papers are full of vivid pictures and graphic details. At the beginning of the Conclave the French cardinals, detained by bad weather, were not present, and much time was lost. " Thus do they delay," says Dandolo, referring to some technical proceedings of the Conclave ; " awaiting these blessed Frenchmen !"‡ When they

* " Venetian Calendar," v., 596.
† *Ibid.* v., 629.
‡ " Questi benedetti Francesi."

did arrive, however, they voted against
Cardinal Pole, on political grounds ; as the
Emperor was known to be keenly anxious
for his election.

Of the three methods of electing a Pope—
by scrutiny, acclamation, and adoration—
the first was followed for some time without
any direct result. No cardinal had a
distinct majority of votes.* "Never were
the times more perilous, or the Conclave
fuller or more divided."† Cardinal Farnese,
a member of the late Pope's family, was
most anxious for Pole's election. On one
occasion, when but two votes were wanting
in his favour, he was perfectly calm, unmoved
either by the prospect of the Pontificate,
or the calumnies which, even in the Vatican,
were whispered against him. Such were
the old absurd charge of heresy, especially
in his leniency as Governor of Viterbo to
Lutherans ; and another wicked and ground-
less accusation, arising out of his great and
secret charity, which was dissipated by
inquiry. A cardinal who was against him
observed to a friend that Pole had no more

* In a " scrutiny " each cardinal records his vote on
paper, which is folded and sealed in a special manner.

† " Venetian Calendar," v., 599.

feeling than a log—being affected neither by ambition, nor by the intrigues against him ! On one occasion, when two-thirds of the votes had been given in his favour, Cardinal Farnese came to his cell, and begged him to receive the Pontificate by " adoration." It was late at night. Pole refused, saying that night and darkness was not the time for such a ceremony, but that it must take place in the morning, after High Mass—always provided that the Conclave was still of the same mind.* Nor could his friend's entreaties move him— wisely, as it turned out ; for in the morning, for some unexplained reason, the imperial delegates voted against Pole, as well as the French representatives, and there could be

* In election by *Acclamation* the principal Cardinal present, addressing the whole Conclave—the scrutinies having failed—asked them to receive as Pope one of their members who had received a large number of votes, and who was generally popular. The Cardinals signified their agreement by greeting the Pope-designate on the spot.

Election by *Adoration* was practically the same, but in this case the assembled cardinals, in order, paid their homage to the new Pope-elect as the first in- timation of his election. It was this third method of settling the difficulty which was suggested by Cardinal Farnese.

then no question of his election. Almost all the cardinals on this day voted for Cardinal Morone, who, after a scrutiny in which he failed by two votes, begged the Conclave to elect Pole. But Pole, who thought far too much time had been lost already, refused a second time. They might now, he said, be more than certain that the Holy Spirit had not elected him ; and in order to leave them greater freedom in their deliberations he would retire, praying and beseeching them to lose no more time over him, but make this holy and necessary election in some other person. His fellow cardinals besought him not to make certain yet that this was God's will. A Conclave was always long, and he could neither assume nor divest himself of the Pontificate at his own will, but only according to that of the Holy Spirit, who alone could guide the election aright. Nevertheless, Pole was now certain that it was not God's will that he should be Pope ; though he refused more than once to give to another cardinal the votes which had been given to him. He had never sought them, nor wanted them ; but he did not think it right to transfer them to some one else.

" The Right Reverend of England," says
Dandolo,* " whose election, should it take
place, may be believed to proceed from God ;
although urged by many of the cardinals
to assist himself on this so great an occasion
. . . answered that he could never utter
one single word, even were his silence to
cost him a hundred lives ; not choosing to
deviate from his ancient maxim which
enjoined him to follow the Lord God, and
to desire nothing but His will." His firm
and unbroken resolution never to seek votes,
even indirectly, was well known even to
those " outside the Vatican."

Meanwhile, the Conclave was suffering
terrible inconveniences. Though many of
the cardinals were old and infirm, on
December 26, 1549, they besought the
officials who supplied them with food
to bring them henceforth only bread
and water—a request which does not
appear to have been granted, as on
January 1, 1550, we find a note that only
" one single dish, roast or boiled " was to
be supplied daily to each member. On
January 22, one of the most famous physicians of the century, Nursia, who appears

* " Venetian Calendar," v., 595.

to have been admitted to attend one of the cardinals, who was ill, threatened the whole Conclave with " plague, or falling sickness," on account of the insanitary condition of the building. Most of them appear to have suffered greatly, but it was not until February 7, 1550, that Cardinal del Monte was elected Pope, with the title of Julius III. This pontiff, the former president of the council of Trent, had for some reason opposed Pole's election ; but as soon as there was a prospect of his being chosen himself he received Pole's warm support. This generosity affected Pope Julius so deeply that he was accustomed to refer to his hostility to the Angelical Cardinal as " the great sin of his life."

The next three years were spent peacefully by Pole between Viterbo, Capranica, and Rome. In 1550, the new Pope commissioned him to draw up the bull for the reassembling of the General Council, but he took very little part in public affairs. The case of England just now was hopeless, he could only pray and wait. He had lost, too, several of his dearest friends, amongst them being Sadolet, and Abbot Cortesio of Venice. At Contarini's death in 1542, he had succeeded that prelate as Cardinal-protector of the Benedictine Order, to which he had always been much attached. During this interval of quiet he sought and obtained permission from Julius III. to retire to Maguzzano, a monastery of that order, situated upon Lake Como ; and to resign his governorship. Here he lived like a religious, delighting in the peace and tranquillity of his beautiful surroundings. Here he revised once more his monumental work *De Unitate*, with the preface intended for Edward VI. ; here too, he gained a measure of health, while leading a life of austerity and strict retirement, in preparation, though he knew it not, for the last great endeavour of his life.

It is in connection with this time that an old writer * says of him : " He was much addicted to prayer, and the contemplation of divine matters. Before he entered Holy Orders he received the Blessed Eucharist on all Sundays, and . . . his chaplain used to relate of him that at Capranica and elsewhere he assisted the priest at the altar, and even put on and took off his vestments, and rendered him, both before and after the sacrifice, all the offices of a menial

* Phillip's " Life of Cardinal Pole," ii., p. 234.

clerk. His accuracy in all the ceremonies and rites of the Liturgy was as observable as the collected air with which he performed them; the very tone of his voice, his countenance, every gesture, spoke of the awe with which he was penetrated, and the attention with which he offered to Almighty God the great sacrifice of atonement and praise; of impetration and thanksgiving."

CHAPTER VIII

THE THIRD LEGATION

1553-1554

ON July 6, 1553, King Edward VI. died; and as soon as he heard the news Pope Julius III. sent Cardinal Pole, at Maguzzano, a brief, dated August 6, appointing him Legate to the new Queen Mary of England; and also to the Emperor, and the King of France, through whose dominions he would pass, and between whom he was, if possible, to make peace. His letters-patent and credentials were to follow; and the appointment of Dr. Pate, the exiled bishop of Worcester and Pole's old friend, as Papal Nuncio, was left to the Legate's discretion.

The rapture of joy which filled his soul overflowed in his letters, which for the next eighteen months give us a graphic picture of the complicated events which led to the Reconciliation.

For it was not by any means plain sailing.

THE THIRD LEGATION

The bitter hostility between the Emperor
and the King of France threatened at any
minute to break into open war; and as
Charles V. desired and intended to marry
Mary to his son Philip II., King of Spain
and Naples, and Pole was believed to be
unfavourable to the match; as also Henry
of France regarded him as a partisan of the
Emperor, whose friend he had always been,
it was abundantly evident that the journey
to England would be fraught with difficulty
and danger. The Cardinal had to pass
through the Emperor's dominions as well
as through France; he was entrusted with
a mission of peace to both monarchs; and
Henry II. was as morally weak as his father
had been. In the end, through political
jealousies, the Legate's journey, as will
appear, was delayed seventeen months;
during which England was in the throes of
rebellion, and an unrest which almost
amounted to civil war.

Before beginning the history of this
eventful journey, one letter, most important
in view of future events must be noticed.
Cardinal Gianpetro Caraffa (who two years
later was to become Pope Paul IV.) had been
created Archbishop of Naples, his native

city, in 1549. He was a furious political
partisan, and in Naples political hatred ran
high against the Emperor and his son
Philip, King of Naples. It is evident from
this letter of Pole's to the Dominican
Master of the Sacred Palace, on August 6,
1553, in which he expresses his joy that
Caraffa is again on affectionate terms with
him, and had expressed a wish to read
De Unitate, that a very serious misunderstanding, fomented by Pole's enemies, had
arisen between them.* It seems probable
from the close of the letter, that Caraffa
had actually paid some attention to the
ridiculous charge of heresy, of which mention
has been made, though the estrangement
was originally, and mainly, political—Pole
being known as a friend of the Emperor,
to whom the Neapolitan Cardinal was
violently opposed.

On August 7 Pole replied at length to the
Pope's letter,† proposing to come to Rome
for an audience before starting on his
mission. On August 13 he wrote the first
of three important letters to the Queen of
England,‡ congratulating her warmly on

* " Venetian Calendar," v., 763.
† *Ibid*, v., 765.   ‡ *Ibid.*, 766.

overcoming so many obstacles and enemies
—rather by supernatural than natural
means, for: "*Spiritus Sanctus supervenit
in corde hominum.*" He points out how
all the evil had originated in the King's
divorce; and speaks of himself as one
"who of all these yet living . . . has suffered
the most, both on this account . . . and
for the Queen's cause." He then tells her
plainly of the necessity of reunion with the
Apostolic See, of which he has been appointed legate; asking her pleasure as to
the time and place of the reconciliation,
for "in this point of obedience to the
Church consists the establishment of her
crown, and the entire welfare of her kingdom." On the same day he received his
legatine commission, through the hands of
Parpaglia, and wrote to Cardinal Dandino,
Papal Legate at Brussels, asking his advice
as to the probable attitude of Charles V.
toward his mission.

At that moment, however, Dandino had
a secret envoy of his own in England, the
future Cardinal Commendone; and on that
very day—August 13, 1553—he was witness
of the scene at Paul's Cross, where an
excited mob threw missiles—one of which

was a dagger—at Dr. Gilbert Bourne, the Queen's chaplain, while he was preaching there. Commendone had a private audience with Queen Mary, who sent a humble message for forgiveness to the Pope ; and returned to Dandino, who, firmly persuaded that the time for Pole's mission had not yet arrived, promptly dispatched him to Rome, to make his report.

A week later, however, Pole wrote directly to the Emperor, informing him of his mission ; begging his help in carrying it out ; and praying for a speedy audience. At the same time the Legate sent a long letter of instructions to the secretary who was to convey his letter to Charles. It seemed impossible, throughout his life, for a man of Pole's transparent sincerity to suspect any one else of double-dealing.

On the 27th, still from the monastery on Lake Como, he wrote his second letter to Mary *—a long and deeply touching epistle. He speaks of the joy with which Catholics everywhere have received the news of her accession ; and the fact that all eyes were fixed on her, who had power to " render the title of the primacy of the Church on

* " Venetian Calendar," v., p. 394.

earth to him to whom the Supreme Head both of Heaven and earth has given it ; " * and reminds her of those who had shed their blood for the primacy ; and her own youthful sufferings, in " the same school in which the Divine Providence which educated you, educated me likewise ; I entering at the same time as you, and learning the same lesson from the same Master." He concludes by urging her to seek, at all costs, the reconciliation of her kingdom.

He wrote, too, to Gardiner † (now Lord Chancellor), referring in most generous terms to that prelate's lapse during the last two unhappy reigns, "not having well learnt at that time . . . the mode of resisting schism," and insisting upon the fundamental truth of papal supremacy. At the same time he begs Gardiner's assistance in the Council, in the great work to which he has been called : " For this, I hope, the Lord God will have elected your lordship as His great and powerful instrument."

On August 30 Parpaglia wrote from

* The Act of Royal Supremacy was not repealed till January, 1555.

† " Venetian Calendar," v., p. 399.

Rome * to say that the Pope left every
detail of the mission entirely in Pole's
hands, with absolute confidence in his
powers ; and thought of recalling his French
and imperial legates, in order that Pole
alone, on his journey to England, might
treat for peace between the two rival
monarchs whose dissensions were the despair
of Christendom. A week later, the Legate,
replying to the Pope, says that he considers
it extremely unfitting that the first session
of the English parliament should pass
without reference being made to re-union,
so that the need of a legate is evident ; and
he asks permission to proceed at once to
the imperial court, *en route* for England.
To his Dominican friend at the Vatican, he
adds, that even if the moment has not yet
come for him to be in England he can at
least be " in the neighbourhood " ; and he
repeats this to Cardinal Dandino at Brussels,†
in a letter flavoured with gentle sarcasm.
He has seen and heard Commendone, he
says ; and is quite agreed on the necessity
of proceeding prudently ; but much experience has shewn him the fatal effects of

* " Venetian Calendar," v., p. 403.
† *Ibid.* v., p. 410.

human respect in a case where the honour
of God was involved ; and in short, he is
ready to face any danger in order to carry
out his mission. On September 10, Queen
Mary, in an audience with the Venetian
ambassador,* let him know "very earnestly,"
that the cardinal should " by no means
come hither, either as a legate or as a private
individual, *until a more fitting time."* She
begged him to assure the Holy Father that
this was not because she had changed her
mind, or that she did not wish to see the
Cardinal, but out of sheer necessity. And
indeed, a woman has seldom been placed
in a more difficult or delicate position.
Before any law could be passed, or repealed
—even that affecting the legitimacy of her
own birth—Parliament must meet ; and
in order that it might, she must first be
crowned. At that ceremony, which took
place on October 1, 1553, she promised to
protect the rights of the Holy See. She
was perfectly aware that in order to do this
effectually she must make an important
political marriage, and that the husband
proposed by her cousin and adviser Charles
V. was unpopular with the nation as a

* " Venetian Calendar," v., 789.

whole. No reliance can be placed on the rumour that she had expressed a wish to Commendone that the Cardinal-deacon might be dispensed from his vows, and marry her himself. But she had not yet seen Philip; the kingdom was rent with religious and civil strife; and she doubtless felt that until the question of her marriage was settled, she could do little towards a public reconciliation with Rome. Such at least was the policy of the Emperor; and it was successful in delaying Pole's journey for a year, lest by any means the marriage of Philip and Mary—to Charles an absolute political necessity—should be frustrated.*

Pole left Maguzzano at the end of September, and wrote to the Pope from Trent on the day of Mary's coronation referring to his hope of establishing peace between Charles and Henry II., to the latter of whom he wrote officially next day; as also to the Constable of France, the Papal Legate, and the Nuncio. On the same day he wrote for the third time to Mary, reminding her of his two former letters, and telling her frankly that the Emperor wished him to

* *See* Gratian's "Life of Commendone," Book iv., p. 144. (Paris, 1699).

defer his mission—which is the advice of a prudent prince, and such as he could recommend Mary to follow, did he not see that she has "always been guided by a greater light than could be given to her by human prudence." He entreats her not to let the first session of Parliament pass before introducing some definite measure of reunion.

To Courtenay, the Marquis of Exeter, he also wrote on the same day, in terms which might perhaps be construed into a wish to see him Mary's husband; which indeed at one time seemed the desire of the nation. On October 8, Mary at length replied to her "good cousin and most blessed Father in Christ," thanking him almost passionately for his kindness and patience, and promising to do all that he wished, as soon as it should be possible to "manifest the whole intent of her heart in that matter." She desires that Parliament may do away with the iniquitous laws which have been the origin of all their afflictions; and then hopes to obtain a general pardon from the Pope.

It was doubtless Pole's generally suspected dislike to the "Spanish match" which caused his detention at Dillingen on his way to an audience with the Emperor. He writes thence* pathetically to the Pope of the " stormy sea " on which he has now embarked ; and of the " mainland of friends " left behind him ; recommending himself earnestly to the Holy Father's prayers.

About this time, Pole's secretary, Pening, whom he had sent with his last letter to the Queen, met the Cardinal at Dillingen, and informed him of the success of his mission. This the Cardinal drew up in the form of a report, which Pening took to the Pope. It informs him that Pening had seen Queen Mary,† who spoke very freely to him, telling him of her desire to be absolved by Cardinal Pole, and that she knew that her coronation ought to be preceded by the General Reconciliation ; but as the latter ceremony was not yet possible she begged Pening to send an express to the Cardinal informing him of her desire, before her crowning, so that she might "remain with her conscience at ease and believe herself absolved." She promised that Parliament should carry out the wishes of the Holy

* October 21, 1553.
† About the middle of September.

Father, so far as she had any power, but that it could not assemble till after her coronation, for which she begged Pening to wait. This he did ; and at the opening of Parliament Gardiner made a fine speech on the unhappy schism of the country. " Her Majesty's final decision was that his Right Reverend Lordship was to come leisurely towards Brussels, where he should await further news."

This was excellent, and Pole's spirits revived. He was now fifty-three ; his health, never robust, had lately begun to fail, and he suffered acutely from rheumatism which often took the form of inflammation of one eye. He must have longed for the peace and tranquillity of his beautiful Benedictine monastery during the next year.

On October 24, the Emperor sent Mendoza to the Legate, to request him to remain for a time where he was. Pole wrote to Charles to remonstrate ; and also to Pope Julius,* to whom he says that, being his legate and owing him his first duty, he will even at his command, disregard the Emperor's wish and go forward. To Mendoza he laid great

* " Venetian Calendar," v., 820.

stress on the indignity offered to a Papal
Legate who was desired to "loiter" in his
progress. Mendoza gave him "clearly to
understand" that the obstruction was the
Spanish marriage. "From this" [says Pole]
"I comprehend that these difficulties about
not allowing me to go forward proceed from
nothing else; and that until the business
be accomplished according to the Emperor's
desire, or his Majesty be altogether quite
certain of being able to conclude it, he
will always find means to prevent my
going; being unable, from what I believe, to convince himself that I would
assist him to place my country in the hands
of a foreigner."

Four days later he addressed a spirited
remonstrance to Charles, on the subject of
his double legation, telling him that it
was not to the honour of any of the parties
concerned that the Cardinal-legate should
be detained, and his audience postponed.

On November 2, Parpaglia returned from
an Embassy to Henry II. at Paris, bringing
good news. The King of France was
delighted to hear of the mission of "his
good cousin and great friend"—(whom he
had as yet never met)—and promising him

a " cordial and honourable " reception in his kingdom.*

A month later Pole wrote a charming letter to Queen Mary, again warning her of the danger to the country as long as it is unreconciled, and reminding her that St. Peter's ship could neither go to pieces nor founder. That as far as England is concerned she is now in the position of the pilot, and responsible for all. It is no time to hesitate. On January 23, 1554, Mary answered this letter, begging Pole to use his legatine powers in providing priests for the realm, confirming in their benefices such as are not " heretics and married priests . . . among whom are certain prelates." She assures him of her longing to see him in England, and has sent the Bishop of Norwich to him, with this letter, to Brussels. A few days later, on January 28, the Cardinal was able to tell the Pope that the Emperor has offered him audience, describing his honourable reception at Brussels, at which Norwich assisted. They had entered in procession, the Bishop of Arras having interviewed the Emperor as to the formal audience ; and making " many apologies "

* " Venetian Calendar," v., 825.

as to Pole's detention at Dillingen, to which, however, the legate did not make " much rejoinder." Beccadelli * tells us that the Cardinal, however, replied : " I own that I was a little surprised that I, who have access to God every day on behalf of the Emperor, should find it so difficult to gain admittance once to the Emperor in the cause of God."

Pole says himself that he was really glad that the Emperor had so far refused to see him, as he had been suffering so terribly from rheumatic gout. He was roused from sleep by the Bishop of Norwich, during the night of February 5, with sudden despatches from England about Wyatt's rebellion. Five days later he had an audience of the Emperor which left matters much as they were. This he describes in a most inter-esting letter to Cardinal del Monte,† in which he refers at great length to the Papal ab-solution which the Holy Father longed to bestow on England, and to the form of Reconciliation. He shall, he says, request the Queen to send him some one who " evinces piety " ; to ask for absolution in the name of the whole nation, so that he

* " Life of Cardinal Pole," p. 145.
† A near relation of the reigning Pope.

may be empowered by England to bestow
it.

On February 12, Mary took the definite
step of presenting twelve of the "most
Catholic" bishops she could find in her
realm to the legate, begging the Pope to
institute and confirm them in their sees—
Pole in the meantime giving them license to
take possession should the Pope's bull not
arrive in time. She calls the Cardinal her
" proctor." *

At Easter Pole was in Paris, where he
had an audience of Henry II. at St. Denis,
and consulted with the great ecclesiastics
and statesmen as to the prospects of peace.
He dined with the King on April 2, 1554;
had another audience, and found Henry
most desirous that hostilities should cease.
On April 8 he made his public entry into
Paris, at the King's request, when he
published the Jubilee. He was back at
Brussels again on April 19, and saw the
Emperor a couple of days later; but on
May 25 came a serious check. The Pope
had been much annoyed by the information that the Emperor's objection to the
Legate's journey arose from Pole's antipathy

* " Venetian Calendar," v., 859.

to the Spanish match. His enemies
had spared no pains to misrepresent facts.
The poor Cardinal writes that he would
rather die than fail to relieve the Pope's
anxiety. His friend Cardinal Morone had
also written to suggest that in all probability
his habitual silence had annoyed the Emperor ; he counselled him not to " lack
demonstration of joy " when the subject
was discussed in future. This Pole very
humbly promises to do to the best of his
ability—acknowledging the fact that hitherto
he has not discussed the Spanish marriage
at all " because it did not seem to him in
conformity with modesty, nor expedient . . .
for the religion which he had in hand, to
speak about such a thing before the persons
concerned had either asked his opinion, or
given him any hint of it." *   Never, perhaps,
had his delicacy and humility appeared to
greater advantage. There is no doubt
that his enemies did him untold harm, both
with the Pope and the Emperor, but secretly.
He compares himself to a man in a field of
long grass, threatened by a deadly snake,
which he cannot see, and at whose movements he can only guess by the moving

* " Venetian Calendar," v., p. 489.

Queen Mary I.

of the grass through which the reptile glides.

The royal wedding took place in Winchester Cathedral on July 25, 1554, and at the beginning of June the Cardinal wrote to the Queen to know if it was her wish that one of his attendants should assist at the ceremony; charging her at the same time to use all her power to make peace between the King of France and the Emperor, who would now be her father-in-law. The Venetian ambassador, Michiel, was eventually chosen to represent the Legate; and on July 11 Pole wrote a courteous letter of congratulation to Philip,* reminding him of his new responsibilities, and of his " inherited title of Catholic."

Of " the most serene Madame Mary, Queen of England and Defendress of the Faith," the retiring Venetian ambassador gives a vivid picture about this time.†

" She is of low stature, with a red and white complexion, and very thin; her eyes are white (? *bianchi*) and large, and her hair reddish; her face is round, with a nose rather low and wide, and were not her age

* " Venetian Calendar," v., 917.
† *Ibid*, v., p. 532.

on the decline she might be called handsome rather than the contrary." To this extremely non-committal opinion he adds: " She is of very spare diet, and never eats until 1 or 2 P.M., although she rises at daybreak, when, after saying her prayers and hearing mass in private, she transacts business incessantly until after midnight, when she retires to rest." He dwells on her attachment to the Church, for which, he says, she is ready to die ; and gives a long list of her accomplishments, including the mastery of five languages. " But she seems to delight above all in arraying herself elegantly and magnificently . . . and she . . . wears much embroidery and gowns and mantles of cloth of gold and cloth of silver of great value. . . . She also makes great use of jewels . . . in which she delights greatly."

This is not, perhaps, the generally received idea of Mary Tudor.

The marriage having been celebrated with great pomp and magnificence, the legate, after waiting a couple of months, addressed a dignified and touching letter of remonstrance to Philip,* which he begins by

* " Venetian Calendar," v., 946.

reminding him it is now a year since he
knocked at his palace gates, and had been
refused admittance. Were the King to
ask " who knocks ? " he would reply : " I
am he, who in order not to exclude your
consort from the palace of England, endured
expulsion from home and country and
twenty years of exile." But this is nothing.
He comes, " not as a private person, but in
the name of the Vicegerent of the King of
kings, the successor of St. Peter ; or rather
of St. Peter himself, who has long been
knocking at the royal gate, which, though
open to others is closed to him alone."
The letter, too long for insertion, is perhaps
one of the most beautiful of this prince
of letter-writers. It was followed on September 28 by one to the Emperor, earnestly
desiring him, now that the marriage is
an accomplished fact, to open the road
to England without further delay.

" If he shall return [to Rome] without
saving his country," the English ambassador
had just written to Queen Mary * from
Brussels, " like as he shall return a sorrowful
man, so shall the realm have lost the fruition

* " State Papers of Queen Mary." Foreign Series,
p. 268. October 5, 1554.

of such a one as for his wisdom, joined with virtue, learning, and godliness, all the world seeketh and adoreth. In whom it is to be thought that God hath chosen a special place of habitation, such is his conversation, adorned with infinite godly qualities above the ordinary sort of men; and whosoever within the realm liketh him worse, I would that he might have with him the talk of one half-hour—it were a right stony heart that within a small time he could not soften. If it be his fortune to depart without shewing the experience thereof in the realm, his going away shall be, in mine opinion, like the story in the gospel of such as dwelt *in regione Geresenorum*, who upon a fond fear, desired Christ, offering Himself unto them, *ut discederet a finibus illorum.*"

His patience was on the point of being rewarded. On October 15 Queen Mary wrote to her " good cousin Pole " by the hand of Simon Renard, the imperial ambassador in England, hoping for his speedy arrival " by God's grace." Philip also wrote, and Pole met Renard at Brussels, to discuss final details; particularly with regard to the legate's instructions as to the restitution of stolen church property, about which the Queen was deeply concerned. Everything being satisfactorily settled, Pole wrote on October 27 to Philip and Mary, informing the latter that his frequent appeals to her ought rather to have been made to the Pope.

There was still an official delay of some days, as it was thought well that the Legate should travel attended by the English ambassador ; * but on November 9 the Bishop of Arras came to Pole from the Emperor. He "exulted and rejoiced," holding in his hand letters from Philip to his father the Emperor, in which he requested that the Legate might set out on his journey at once, but begging him to arrive un-officially ; though he should be subsequently publicly recognised as Legate by King, Queen and nation. The King earnestly requested him not to go into detail as to the distribution of church property, but to "announce good intentions to all in general terms."

The first stipulation was a disappointment "such as is wont to happen in all the affairs of God ; " but Pole promised to fall in with

* Sir John Masone.

their wishes, " not unwillingly ; " and as to the second item, " very willingly."

All preparations being now finished he left Brussels, escorted by Lord Edward Hastings and Lord Paget, on the 13th, and, in less than a week, reached Calais, where he was received with great rejoicings. On his arrival it was remarked with awe that the contrary wind which had raged for some days, suddenly dropped, and became fair.

He crossed the Channel to Dover in the royal yacht, escorted by six men of war; and on November 24, 1554, the exile of twenty-three years set foot in his native land.

CHAPTER IX

THE RECONCILIATION
1554–1556

AFTER a prosperous voyage the legate was met at Dover by his nephew, Lord Montague (son of his eldest brother, beheaded 1538), the Bishop of Ely, and a train of noblemen who were commissioned to escort him with all state to the King and Queen. All along the road to Canterbury people flocked to see him and receive his blessing ; the streets of all the villages were lined with men and women, kneeling and weeping. At Rochester his friend Pate, Bishop of Worcester, who had preceded him by some weeks, met him with a message from Mary (who was evidently reassured as to the state of the country), beseeching him to a sume henceforth the state of Papal Legate, for as such she intended to receive him.

At Gravesend, on November 23, he was approached by a great deputation of nobles, who handed him the copy of an Act, sealed with a golden seal, passed only the day before,* by which the Attainder passed on him and his family was reversed, and all his rights and privileges of nobility restored to him. His letters-patent to exercise his legatine commission in England were also handed to him. The Cardinal was deeply moved. We can only dimly guess what his home-coming was to Reginald Pole—the reaping in joy of what he had sown in suffering beyond all tears. He entered the royal barge, which was in waiting. At the prow was fixed his silver legatine cross, surmounting a tall staff. All the way up the river, where the crowded craft left a broad way for the legate's triumphal progress, the people welcomed him with cheers. There could be no doubt as to the passionate thankfulness of England as a whole.

So swift was his progress on a favourable tide that, before it was expected, the clustering thousands lining the banks at Lambeth and Westminster saw the silver cross shine far down the river in the misty dimness of the November afternoon. Philip and Mary

* It passed through the House of Commons three times in one day.

awaited the legate at Whitehall, and as the royal barge swung up amid a roar of welcome, the King, the Chancellor, and a retinue of nobles descended the steps to the water's edge to meet him.

" Your Majesty is going to wait on your subject ? " said one of the lords-in-waiting. " The King is going to receive the Legate of the King of kings," replied Philip gravely.

At the head of the stairs the Queen awaited him, and saluted him with feelings which can be imagined rather than described. After a short conference, during which some presentations were made, and the Legate displayed his credentials from the Pope, he re-entered his barge, and was conducted in state by the Chancellor to the Archbishop's palace at Lambeth, on the opposite bank of the river (vacated by Cranmer, now in prison as a traitor), which had by Mary's command been prepared for him and his suite.

Beccadelli and his devoted friend Priuli were with him, together with a large retinue, and the former gives us some graphic details of the events of the next few days. From his descriptions and from those of another eye-witness we can form a vivid picture of what took place.

THE ANGELICAL CARDINAL

" [Cardinal Poole] of late is arrived in Englande as ambassadour and legate from the Pope's holynes, with most ample commission to receave the realme of Englande unto the unitie of the Church. . . . He is and seemeth to be of nature sad and grave, whose good life may be an example to the reste of his profession, and his excellent learning is well knowen through all Europe. . . . For it is commonly sayde of him by lerned men in Rome, and in other places where I have travayled, ' *Polus cardinalis, natione Anglus, pietatis et literarum testimonio dignus, non qui Polus Anglus, sed qui Polus Angelus vocetur.*' " *

At Lambeth he rested after the fatigues and emotions of his journey ; but on the third day went to court, and on the day following received the King at Lambeth. During these two interviews everything was arranged for the public reconciliation. On November 28 the Legate attended the House of Lords, in company with the King and Queen. The Commons being summoned to the bar, Pole addressed the whole assembly, after he had been briefly intro-

* Letter of John Elder, *circa* 1555. Camden Society, 1850 (from which the following quotations are taken).

duced by the Lord Chancellor, who concluded by begging for " attente, and an inclynable eare to him."

" When his lordship had thus made an end, my lord Cardinall, taking the occasion offred, without any studye, as it seemed, spake in effect as foloweth : "

Referring in touching words to his five-and-twenty years exile he thanked them for reinstating him in his rights of nobility. " Yf the offer of my service might have been receaved, it was never to seke : and where that could not be taken you never failed of my prayer, nor never shall." Yet this nobility, he reminded them, was but earthly, and he was there to reinstate them as citizens of a Heavenly country. After a sketch of the benefits which England had from the beginning received from the Apostolic See, and a review of the miserable events of the past, in which he pointed out that heresy inevitably results from schism, he came to the purpose of his mission. " When all lyghte of true religion seamed utterly extincte, as the churches defaced and aulters overthrowen, the ministers corrupted ; even lyke as in a lampe the lyghte being covered, yet it is not quenched, even so in a few remained the confession of Christ's fayth. . . . And therefore it may be sayd : *Da gloriam Deo.*" He spoke feelingly of the Queen, and her Catholic marriage ; " in which respecte greate cause you have to gyve thankes to Almighty God that hathe sent you such Catholyke governours ; " and most gracefully and charitably of the King's father, the Emperor. He spoke of the twofold division of power, spiritual and temporal, the Author of all power being Almighty God. The " King and Quene's Majesties " represented the power temporal, " committed to them immediatelye from God. . . . The other power is of ministracyon, whyche is the power of the Keies, which is by the authoritie of God's worde . . . geven to the Apostolike Sea of Rome. . . . From which sea I am here deputed legate . . . and have the keyes committed to my hands. I confess to you that I have the keyes not as mine own keyes, but as the keyes of him that sent me, and yet cannot open, not for want of power in me to gyve, but for certayne impédimentes in you to receave, whiche must be taken awaye before my commission can take effect. . . I cum not to destroy but to build. I cum to reconcyle, not to condemne. I cum not to compel but to call againe. I am not cum to call anything in question already done, but my commission is of grace and clemencye . . . for touchinge all matters that be past, they shal bee as thinges cast into the sea of forgetfulnes. But the meane wherby you shall receave this benefit is to revoke and repeale those lawes and statutes whiche be impedymentes, blockes, and barres to the execution of my commission." He compared his own position, unable to return to England until the Act passed against him was revoked, to theirs, who could not receive the Papa absolution until the "abrogacion of such lawes whereby you have disjoyned and dissevered yourselves from the unity of Christe's Church"; and he concluded by begging them "lyke true Christians and provydente men" to consider their position and take such steps to remedy it as might tend to the glory of God and the welfare of their country.

"This was the substannce of my lord cardinalles oration, or rather his tale, which he pronounsed in such sort as no man could judge it any studyed matter, but a thing spoken *ex tempore*. Wherof a frende of myne beinge a burges of the parliamente, and presente at the same tyme, toke the notes, and gave me the same in writing, so (as I beleve) nothing that he spoke in effecte is omitted."

He was heard in thrilling silence, broken now and then by sobs. After so many years the awful strain was loosed. To the aching hearts of those who had sinned through pride or terror, ignorance or fear, came a passion of repentance for their sins as a nation, which rose like a sea, the beating of whose waves might almost be heard.

Then Gardiner rose, and in a voice choked with emotion thanked the Legate for his " good offices to the nation " ; after which Pole withdrew " to hys house at Lambeth " ; and Parliament listened to a fervent speech from the Chancellor, in which, as one himself guilty of schism, he implored his brethren to return to the unity of Christ's Church, as in all humility he willed to do himself.

Next day Parliament met again, and in both Houses the question was put as to whether it was desired to return to the communion of the Catholic faith as a nation ; and whether it was agreed that the schismatic laws should be repealed. The motion was carried through both Houses, with one dissentient * in the Commons; and a resolution † was passed to beg the Cardinal to bestow upon them the pardon of the Pope.

The next day was fixed for the Reconciliation of England. It was St. Andrew's Day,‡ November 30, 1554; a day subsequently ordered to be kept for ever sacred in England.

A dazzling company of prelates and nobles—six bishops and six knights of the garter—escorted the Cardinal-legate across

* Sir R. Bagnall, who conscientiously objected on the ground of having sworn to the laws of Henry VIII.

† "A Supplication, 'whereby this realm and dominion might be again united to the Church of Rome by means of the Lord Cardinal Poole,' from Lords and Commons." (Journal of House of Commons. November 29, 1554.)

‡ "*Ultimo Novembris in Festo Sancti Andreæ*. At Afternoon, before the King's and Queen's Majesties at the Palace, the Lords and Commons being present, the Supplication was read in *Latin*, and exhibited by their Majesties to the Lord Legate; who, making an Oration of great joy, that was for the return of the lost sheep, did, by the Pope's Holiness's Authority, give Absolution to this whole realm, and the Dominion of the same." (Journal of the House of Commons. November 30, 1554.)

the river to Whitehall, where, in the great
Chamber of the Palace, says Beccadelli,
the House of Lords was bidden to assemble,
and the Commons summoned.

There under a gorgeous canopy of jewelled
cloth of gold, upon a daïs magnificent with
hangings of royal tapestry, Philip and Mary
awaited the Cardinal-legate, whom they
received with the deepest respect, as he
arrived " in full pomp," in his splendid
crimson robes—all the insignia of his Legateship, the silver cross, pillars, and axes being
borne before him. No pageants, as it has
been often said, can equal those of the
Catholic Church. He took his seat on the
Queen's right hand, the King being on her
left, and rather nearer to her ; and there
was a moment's silence, as the murmur of
wonder and welcome died away, and the
Chancellor rose to make his speech. They
remembered, he said, what had been agreed
upon the day before. Were they still of
the same mind ; and did they desire to
ratify it ? And then arose a heartfelt cry :
" We do—we do."

Then Gardiner, turning to the King and
Queen, presented a petition from the nation
declaring the sorrow of the people for their

schism, and for the enactments against
Rome, all of which they now purposed to
annul, beseeching from the Legate pardon
and restoration.

Philip and Mary read it—the Queen
through blinding tears—and then the Chancellor read it aloud so that all could hear.
Then the whole assembly rose as one
man to its feet and advanced as near as
possible to the Legate, while the Queen,
kneeling, besought him in her name and the
King's to grant the pardon for which they
sued.

Again there was a silence, choked with
sobs, while the Legate, with a gesture,
motioned them all to their seats, and then
proceeded to address them. How thankful
should they not be, as Englishmen, for
God's mercy to their country, to which He
had given so signal a proof of His love, in
sending repentance to the whole kingdom.
"If the angels in Heaven," said the quiet
voice, "rejoice over the conversion of a
single sinner, what must be their joy to-day
at the sight of a whole kingdom which
repenteth ? "

Then as he rose to his feet, the whole
assembly fell on their knees, and a threefold

cry for pardon went up. All eyes were centred on the slight, dignified figure, with his grave clear eyes and face marked by suffering, standing there in his trailing scarlet robes—the representative of St. Peter himself sent to reconcile England—and then he raised his hand, with the great jewel flashing from it. The words of absolution fell like rain into their parched souls.

" Dominus Noster Jesus Christus, qui nos suo pretioso sanguine redemit, et mundavit ab omnibus peccatis et iniquamentis nostris, ut exhiberet sibi sponsam gloriosam, non habentem maculam, neque rugam, quem et Pater constituit caput super omnem ecclesiam, ipse per suam misericordiam vos absolvat. Et nos auctoritate apostolica per sanctissimum dominum nostrum Julium papam tertium, eius vices in terris gerentem, nobis concessa, vos et unumquemque vestrum, et regnum universum, et eius dominia ab omni haeresi, et schismate, et quibusvis sententiis, censuris et poenis propterea incursis absolvimus et liberamus et unitati sanctae matris ecclesiæ restituimus; prout in literis nostris plenius continebitur. In nomine Patris ✠ et Filii ✠ et Spiritus Sancti ✠ Amen." *

And, as they wept, the people cried again, Amen. But no one—not even those who receive the hundredfold now in this present time—can know what that supreme moment was to Reginald Pole.

They sang *Te Deum* afterwards, in the Chapel Royal, tears of joy running down their faces.

The "Supplycacion" for pardon, from the nation to the Legate, is too interesting to be overlooked. It begins by a declaration that Lords and Commons, representing the

---

* Our Lord Jesus Christ, who with His most precious blood hath redeemed and washed us from all our sins and iniquities, that He might purchase unto Himself a glorious spouse without spot or wrinkle, and whom the Father hath appointed Head over all His Church ; He by His mercy absolve you. And we, by the Apostolic authority given to us by the most holy Lord Pope Julius III. His Vicegerent on earth, do absolve and deliver you, each and all, together with this whole realm and the dominions thereof, from all heresy and schism, and from all and every judgment, censures and pains for that Cause incurred.. And also we do restore you again unto the unity of our Holy Mother Church, as in our letters more plainly it shall appear. In the name of the Father ✠ and of the Son ✠ and of the Holy Ghost ✠ Amen.

whole realm, beg the King and Queen to present their petition to the Cardinal, and continues, " we dooe declare ourselves very sorye and repentante of the scisme and disobedyence . . . agaynste the . . . Sea Apostolyke, either by making laws against the supremacy of the sayed Sea, or otherwise dooing or speakynge that might impugn the same." They promise, to the uttermost of their power, to abrogate and repeal all laws against Rome ; begging Philip and Mary, as persons " undefiled in the offence of thys body towards the saide Sea," so to set forth this their suit to the Legate that they may obtain " from the Sea Apostolike, by the saide most reverend father, as well particularlye as universallye, *absolution, release,* and *discharge* from all danger of such censures and sentences, as by the lawes of the church we be fallen in. And that we maye, as children repentaunte, be received into the bosome and unitie of Christe's Churche. So as thys noble realme, wyth all the membres thereof, maye in unitie and perfecte obedience to the Sea Apostolike, and popes for the tyme beinge, serve God and your majesties to the furderance and advancemente of hys honoure and glorye. Amen."

THE RECONCILIATION

On December 1, the Lord Mayor of London waited on the Legate, desiring him to make a triumphal procession through the city, which he did two days later.

"Then the fyrste Sundaye in Advente followinge, my lorde cardinall came, at tenne of the clocke, from Lambeth by water, and landed at Pole's * wharfe. And cumminge from thence to Pole's churche † with a crosse, ii. pyllers, and two pollaxes of sylver borne before hym, he was there receaved by my lorde chaunceller, with procession. Where he taryed untill the kynge's cummynge; whose hyghnes came from Westminster by lande, and all hys nobles before hym, to Pole's also, at a leven of the clocke. And so the kynge's majestie and my lorde Cardinall, with all the lordes of the privye counsell beinge presente, with suche an audience of people as was never sene in that place before, my lorde chaunceller entered Pole's crosse. And after that the people ceased, that so much as a whisperinge could not be hearde amongest them, more than amongest those of whom the

* Paul's.

† The old Cathedral of St. Paul's, destroyed in the Great Fire, 1666.

poet Virgil speaketh, *Conticuere omnes,
intentique ora tenebant,** but every bente
hartelye wyth eares to here, eyes to perceave,
and handes to wryte, his lordship proceded,
and tooke to hys theam † these wordes of
the epystle of that daye, wrytten by Saynte
Paule the holye apostle in the xiii. chapter
to the Romaynes, *Fratres, scientes quia hora
est jam nos de somno surgere, &c.*, whyche
parcelle of Scripture was so godlye and so
clearkelye handeled by him, as no manne
alyve . . . was able to meande it."

Gardiner, in a most able sermon, informed
his hearers of facts which few, to-day,
perhaps realise. He told them that Henry
VIII. had twice intended to make his
submission, the first time eighteen years
before, at the time of the northern rising ;
and later on sending Gardiner himself to the
Emperor, to ask him to be his intercessor
with the Pope : " but it tooke none effecte
because the time was not." At the beginning of Edward's reign, again there was
talk of submission, to which the council did
not agree, lest it should be said the realm
was unable to defend itself during the King's

* " Æneid," ii., l. 1.
† Theme.

minority without the Pope's assistance! Lastly, Queen Mary, at her coronation, had earnestly desired to restore the Pope's supremacy, "but the tyme . . . was not then."

" These, wyth manye other notable, yea, lamentable lessons, to longe here to bee rehersed, hys lordshyppe then declared, whyche moved a greate nombre of the audience with sorrowfull syghes and wepynge teares to chaunge theyr cheere." At the end, after dwelling upon Cardinal Pole's mission, and speaking with deep gratitude of the action of the King and Queen, the Bishop told the people that if they remembered their promises, and " hartely embraced and faithfully followed [them] they al then myghte synge with the angell whiche appered to the shepherds at the natyvytie and birth of oure Savioure, Jesus Christ, *Gloria in excelsis Deo et in terra pax hominibus*. And finally to say with the prophet and psalmist David, *Haec est dies quam fecit Dominus, exultemus et laetemur in ea.*"

The sermon was preached after solemn High Mass had been sung in the presence of the Cardinal-legate, the King, Queen, and the whole court. " Syns the day of whiche sermon all such thinges as were amis and out of order here begin now to cum to rule and square, and occupye their auncyente and accustomed places."

On the following Thursday Convocation assembled, and kneeling, humbly entreating pardon, was solemnly absolved. A fortnight later the ancient Heresy Acts, which it had suited Henry VIII. to repeal, were re-enacted; just after an act had been passed restoring jurisdiction to the clergy.

But the principal question which troubled the kingdom was the restoration of abbey lands and church property. By far the greater part—nearly three-quarters—of this had been confiscated to the crown by Henry VIII., and this wholesale plunder Philip and Mary gladly agreed to restore. But even then an enormous amount was in the hands of private persons, to whom, and to whose fathers, it had been granted by the King for services rendered, or for some caprice; and such persons, though most desirous of returning to the church, were not in all cases equally desirous of giving up their wealth. It was this difficulty, clearly foreseen by Philip's acute mind, which had caused him to delay the Legate's reception up to the moment of his leaving Brussels, whither he had sent Renard to treat fully of the question. It would have been most unwise to press the nation as to the spoils of the church, just as it was returning bodily to its allegiance, and Pole gladly consented to grant delay to allow of the matter being arranged by degrees. A large number, however, gave up their lands and money to safeguard those who did not wish to do so ; and by an Act passed on January 3, 1555, such possessions were granted to their holders, with the Legate's full consent. Pope Paul IV. subsequently, at Pole's request, granted a bull confirming this, on September 16, 1555.

His letters to the Pope (Julius III.) at this time, are alive with interest. On the day of Reconciliation he wrote to him, giving a detailed description of all that had taken place. Philip, too, who had been deeply moved, wrote on the same day to the Holy Father, whose delight at hearing the news was expressed by public rejoicings, after a solemn *Te Deum* sung in St. Peter's. King Henry of France wrote to congratulate Pole, who had by no means lost sight of the second half of his legation, and was even then discussing a plan by which peace might be secured between France and the Empire.

Meanwhile on the Feast of the Conversion of St. Paul (January 25) there was a general procession of the Blessed Sacrament, with representatives from every parish in London, in which took part 150 to 200 priests and religious, with the members of the City Guilds and " singing men," preceded by the children of the Greyfriars and St. Paul's Schools, all singing " *Salve Festa Dies.*" Eight mitred bishops followed, Bonner, the Bishop of London, bearing the Blessed Sacrament ; the procession being closed by the Lord Mayor, aldermen and guildsmen. The King and Cardinal were present in the cathedral, and in the evening, amid general rejoicing, bonfires were lit, and the whole city of London was illuminated.

The Queen sent representatives of the three estates of the realm—the Bishop of Ely, Lord Montague and Sir Edward Carne, —to Rome with a letter of introduction to the Pope from Cardinal Pole. Scarcely had they started, however, when news came of the death of Pope Julius III., on March

23, 1555; and of the succession to the Pontificate of Pope Marcellus II., a most holy and learned prelate, and a personal friend of Pole's, who unhappily only survived his election by three weeks. Pole's own name had again been mentioned as that of the future Pope, but owing to his absence or, more probably, Cardinal Caraffa's influence, he was not so near election as during the last conclave.

When the ambassadors reached Rome, two pontiffs having died during their long journey, they were received by Pope Paul IV., formerly Cardinal Caraffa, entering Rome on the very day of his coronation. Paul IV. embraced them publicly, and was so delighted with the importance of the embassy, and the graceful and eloquent Latin oration of the Bishop of Ely, that he wrote himself to Philip and Mary, to express his pleasure and to send his blessing. As to the Cardinal-legate, nothing, said Paul IV., that he or Philip or Mary could ever do would be anything but unequal to Pole's marvellous virtue and heroic qualities. In view of future events, it is well to remember this.

In the spring Pole was very ill. The cause

may have been the damp climate, to which for so long he had been unaccustomed, but on April 15 the Venetian ambassador writes : *
" Cardinal Pole's indisposition increased so violently, a malignant fever having never left him for five consecutive days, that not only his own attendants, but the physicians themselves despaired of his life ; and the former being even more tender and apprehensive than the latter, their extreme affliction and dismay, especially that of Monsignor Priuli, was too piteous a sight ; but through the aid and grace of the Almighty his right reverend lordship is not only better, but out of danger, having already passed four days without fever, though so weak and exhausted that all who see him well know how much he must have suffered. He is now intent on taking rest and gaining strength that he may be able, if necessary, to cross the Channel for this Conference." This was part of his plan for peace, to which reference has been made. In the same letter the ambassador mentions the horrible outrage on Easter Sunday at St. Margaret's, Westminster, when the priest, while giving Holy Communion during Mass, was attacked by

* " Venetian Calendar," vi., 57.

a violent fanatic with a drawn sword, who wounded him so terribly on the head and hands that his life was despaired of. His blood fell into the chalice.

A few weeks later the Cardinal was sufficiently recovered to preside at the Conference which, after much preliminary negotiation, Henry II. had agreed to hold at Marc, near Calais, with representatives of the Emperor. To make peace between these monarchs had been one of the great endeavours of Pole's life, and it was indeed part of his legatine commission. Queen Mary was intensely anxious as to the result, and had used all her influence with her father-in-law, the Emperor, and the King of France, to bring about the meeting. The first session was held in May, 1555, and the Legate used all his powers of persuasion and diplomacy ; but political jealousy was too strong, and on June 8, a month later, the Conference was broken up ; any hope of an agreement between Charles and Henry being out of the question, as both parties insisted on concessions which neither side would grant.*

* *See* letter of the Constable of France to French Ambassador, "Venetian Calendar," vi., 114, and of Venetian Ambassador, *ibid.*, 204.

It was a terrible grief to Pole, who, however, in the difficult and generally thankless position of arbitrator had greatly endeared himself to both parties ; and, indeed, for many years it would have been difficult to find a man more universally loved and revered than Cardinal Pole. Not one who knew him personally, not even one who had studied his life in his letters, could accuse him, as Protestants have not hesitated to do, of cruelty, during the prosecutions for heresy now beginning in England. The question of the so-called " Marian persecution " of heretics cannot be fully discussed here, any more than the wholesale butchery of Catholics which took place during the two previous reigns. They were the methods of the age. It must never be forgotten that the greater number of Protestants who suffered under Mary were put to death as traitors as well as heretics ; and most had assisted at the martyrdom of Catholics—all certainly would joyfully have done so had the tables been turned. Many of them had urged the assassination of the Queen, and plotted against her ; and all of them had uttered foul and shocking blasphemies about holy things. All, without exception, at the beginning of the reign, were invited, and in some cases compelled to leave England, and not one was put to death without repeated efforts to save him by reconciliation with the Church.* At the same time, the heroic courage of these martyrs to private judgment must in many

* " For political offences men were slaughtered by hundreds and thousands in the sixteenth century ; and the very historians who compassionate those who were slain for their religious principles, under the notion that the religious party to which they are opposed is discredited thereby, are among the first to vindicate the severity which they represent as necessary to preserve the peace of society.

" If we credit [the utterly discredited] Foxe, the martyrologist, there was a parcel of bloodthirsty men at the head of society, or rather at the head of the Christian Church in this country, whose only object was to delight their cruel hearts by witnessing the agonies of their fellow creatures. Such persons there may have been . . . but we may doubt whether they existed in greater numbers in the sixteenth than in the nineteenth century. If we look to the facts of history, we find, at the commencement of Mary's reign, that there was no desire or intention to deal harshly with the reformers, whether Protestant or Calvinist. . . . [their] number was small, they were aware of their danger . . . [and] every facility was . . . afforded them for quitting the country."—Hook. " *Lives of the Archbishops of Canterbury.*" Vol. viii., p. 358.

Such words as these, from so intensely Protestant a writer as Dr. Hook are worthy of careful consideration.

cases arouse our admiration. Cranmer, Ridley and Latimer had been allowed to dispute at Oxford with certain Catholic divines, one of whom, the Bishop of Gloucester, said " Latimer leaneth to Cranmer, Cranmer to Ridley, and Ridley to the singularity of his own wit." *

Cardinal Pole had exhorted the Bishops in Convocation, in January, 1555, to use gentleness rather than harshness to heretics ; but they, who had suffered cruel persecution, and been in danger at the hands of a king whose only law was his own will, can scarcely be wondered at for employing, to stamp out the hated heresy which his acts had fostered, means which were at least strictly legal. Had not they, too, tasted the bitterness of separation ? Heresy, implying wilful separation from the Church was mortal sin, and the death of the body was to be preferred to that of the soul.

Latimer, an old man with a harsh and bitter tongue, who had, to quote his own words to Cromwell, " played the fool " † at the burning of the Blessed John Forrest, was burnt at the same stake as Ridley at

* Gairdner. " History of the English Church in the Sixteenth Century," p. 338. † Preached.

Oxford, on October 16, 1555. Both these men were apostate, married priests ; and though the Legate had on September 28 sent three Bishops to Oxford to examine them, and if anyhow possible to obtain their submission and consequent pardon, both were obdurate.

Three months before, on June 4, there was published with the sanction of the Legate, and of Convocation, a prayer book for general use in the realm. It was called : " an uniforme and Catholyke primer in Latin and Englishe, withe manye godlye and devoute prayers, newly set forth by ceartayne of the cleargye with the assente of the moste reverende father in God, the lorde cardinall Pole hys grace." It consisted of morning and night prayers, the Jesus Psalter, and prayers of St. Bridget on the Passion, " Matyns of oure Ladye," office of the dead, and form of examination of conscience before confession, together with short meditations on the Passion.

At the end of August, 1555, King Philip left England for Brussels, where his father the Emperor was about to make over to him formally his Spanish dominions. The Queen felt the parting keenly, her only comfort being in the fact that the King, on leaving, recommended her to the Cardinal's care, charging him to watch over and cheer her ; at the same time bidding the Council do nothing without the Legate's express sanction. He was, in fact, Prime Minister of England, or would have been, had he not gently but firmly refused to meddle in temporal things. He promised to receive reports, and advise when necessary, but not more. In accordance with the wish of Philip and Mary, he took up his residence at the royal palace of Greenwich, where he could be in constant attendance on the Queen. To this palace was attached a Friary of Franciscan observants, lately reinstated by Mary.

It was perhaps at this time that the first apprehension of real danger clouded Pole's path. Pope Paul IV., a man of blameless and even austere life, was a violent political partisan, as has been already said. In September, 1555, he had a serious misunderstanding with the Emperor, in which Pole addressed an earnest letter of remonstrance to the Pope, who had been on the point of plunging Europe into a terrible war. It is probable that the Legate's intervention revived in Paul IV.'s mind the dislike and distrust of Pole which he had already manifested as Archbishop of Naples ; with results which very soon were to declare themselves.

On November 4, the Legate convened a synod at Whitehall, during which he expressed his satisfaction with the fervour and zeal of the bishops and clergy, and their exemplary lives. After Mass of the Holy Ghost sung in the chapel of the Palace royal, they proceeded to discuss the redistribution of the abbey lands, according to the wish of the Holy Father, to whom Pole wrote a full account of their proceedings.* On November 12, Gardiner died ; and Pole, in deploring his loss to Philip and Mary, remarks " how necessary it is to supply his place with one not merely a Catholic by name," one that should " shew himself less harsh and stern, but no less firm and ardent " than the dying Bishop.

The anniversary of the Reconciliation, November 30, 1555, was kept with great solemnity. The synod was still sitting, and its chief work was the enactment on February 10, 1556, of a new code of con-

* " Venetian Calendar," vi. (i.), 270.

stitutions drawn up by the Cardinal, entitled : " *Reformatio Angliæ, ex Decretis Reginaldi Poli.*" There were twelve decrees.

(1) Concerning the thanks to be daily given to God in the celebration of the Mass, for the return of this kingdom to the unity of the Church, and concerning the annual celebration of the memory of that event.

(2) Respecting ordinances and opinions, the reception and rejection of books, and the public teaching of the Canon law. (This dwells strongly on the Primacy, and treats very beautifully of the seven sacraments, ordering Reservation in every parish church.)

(3) Concerning the residence of bishops and other clerks. (Non-residence strongly censured.)

(4) That bishops and others exercising the cure of souls should preach to the people ; and that parish priests should instruct children in the elements of the faith.

(5) Concerning the lives of the clergy.

(6) Respecting the examination of candidates for Holy Orders.

(7) Respecting the provision of ecclesiastical benefices (which were not to remain empty).

(8) That there be no grants of the rights of presentation or of advowsons permitted ... contrary to the ordinance of the sacred canons.

(9) Concerning simony.

(10) Concerning the non-alienation of church property ; making an inventory of chattels ; * not farming church appointments.

(11) Of the diocesan seminaries which it was desirable to form at each cathedral.

(12) Concerning the visitation of churches. (Strict orders were given as to parochial visitations, especially as regards the Blessed Sacrament.)

The prelates, by a re-enactment of a statute of Pope Innocent III., were to correct their clergy "without appeal."

Meanwhile on December 4, 1555, sentence of excommunication was pronounced by Paul IV. against Cranmer, who had utterly failed to justify himself of the charges of heresy which he had been allowed a period of eighty days to answer. He was at Oxford, and not then in prison. By Pole's courtesy he had been removed from Bocardo

---

* A convenient term for movables of almost every sort, including, according to some old writers, even a wife, as part of the household goods.

to the house of the Dean of Christ Church, and there, on February 12, 1556, he was degraded by a Papal commission of two bishops * from his offices of Archbishop, priest, and all the minor orders one by one—appealing passionately to the next general council, though it was by the decrees of that still sitting under which he suffered—and was handed over to the secular power, plain Thomas Cranmer, apostate priest and hopeess heretic.

During his imprisonment he wrote and signed no less than six " Recantacyons," † by which he hoped his life might have been saved ; but in the great doctrine of Transubstantiation it was impossible for him to believe. Finding therefore that the six recantations availed nothing, he made at the last moment a seventh, retracting the previous ones, and declaring he had written them against his own belief, in the hope of saving his life. After asking for prayers for his soul after his death the unfortunate man, with the courage of despair, died by fire on Saturday, March 21, 1556.

* Bonner and Thirlby.

† *See* a most interesting Latin pamphlet discovered in 1682 in Paris, " Bishop Cranmer's Recantacyons," republished by Houghton and Gairdner.

He had been the chief instrument in "dissolving" the marriage between Henry VIII. and Katherine ; and in declaring the present Queen illegitimate. The natural weakness of his character had been warped by his ambition, and he had lent himself, a willing tool in every new development of Henry's mad ambition. "He died a martyr's death," says his sympathetic historian, Hook, who, however, adds : "but to die bravely when death is inevitable is not sufficient to constitute a martyr." "On Saturday last," writes the Venetian ambassador,* "Cranmer . . . was burned, having fully verified the opinion formed of him by the Queen, that he had feigned recantation, thinking thus to save his life, and not that he had received any good inspiration ; so she considered him unworthy of pardon."

On the day before Cranmer's death, Reginald Pole was ordained priest in the Greyfriars' Church attached to the palace at Greenwich, by the Archbishop of York, the Bishop of London, and five other bishops of the southern province, the Queen being present, and the church filled with a great congregation, all of whom were deeply

* "Venetian Calendar," vi. (i.), 434.

affected. The next day, Saturday, the Feast of St. Benedict he said his first Mass in the same church, with intense devotion, and on the following Sunday morning, March 22, 1556, was consecrated by the same prelates Archbishop of Canterbury, of which See he had already been appointed administrator.

On Monday, 23, he took the oath of allegiance to the Pope " in the parlour of the convent," and two days after, on the Feast of the Annunciation, which fell this year in Passion week, he received the pallium in the parish church of Our Lady of Arches, at Bow, which was " hung with cloth of gold and rich arras,"* and splendidly decorated. Entering with a procession of clergy, among whom were six bishops, he was presented by a member of the congregation with a petition begging for a sermon, to test—as many have supposed— his real powers of extempore preaching. The Bishop of Worcester sang the Mass, and after the Gospel the Cardinal-Archbishop turned to the people and spoke to them simply and eloquently of three things— mission, apostolic succession and unity.

* Hook.

He explained to them what the pallium meant—made not of silk and jewels, but of plain white wool, to symbolise that all power and authority came from the Lamb of God. He who above all else loved peace, spoke of it with such intense feeling that he and all his audience were moved to tears, as one of them relates.* ' "And thus" (he exclaimed) . . . "would ye but know the great grace God grants you by the mission of this peace ! " On uttering these words his right reverend lordship could not restrain his tears, and after using that expression "would ye but know," he stayed himself for a moment, and then adding . . . "what God grants you," remained silent for a short while, his eyes being suffused with tears.

· " This peace, then, which I am come to offer you on the part of God, must be received by those who wish for its enjoyment with great humility, as did on this day the glorious Virgin, who when the Angel announced peace to her in these words *" Ave Maria gratia plena, Dñus. tecum,"* replied " *ecce ancilla Domini* " . . . without any doubt at all, and with the utmost

* " Venetian Calendar," vi. (i.), 432–4.

humility [receiving] the peace offered to her. . . . By imitating her you also will come to a peace truly blessed. *Beati pacifici, quoniam ipsi filii Dei vocabuntur."* A sermon, concludes the ambassador who quotes it, which though unprepared, bore good fruit during the Holy Week.

He was now chief adviser to the Queen and Council, virtual Prime Minister of England, Archbishop of Canterbury, Cardinal, and Papal Legate. To no one—not to St. Thomas of Canterbury himself—had so dazzling a position been granted. Truly to Reginald Pole was granted the hundredfold—now, in this present time !

CHAPTER X

THE GREAT VICTORY

1556–1558

REGINALD POLE did not die in a
blaze of glory. God had yet in store
for him the greatest trial of his life—
the final test by which his beautiful soul
was tried and perfected and released. We
are not called upon to understand, much
less explain, why these inexplicable events
were allowed to take place. We can only
believe, as he did, that they were permitted
by Almighty God for His glory, and the
perfection through suffering of His servant.

Almost the first act of the new Archbishop was to " set up with Black Friars "
the church of St. Bartholomew the Great,
in Smithfield. The return of the banished
religious was a subject both he and Mary
had much at heart, and 1556 saw many
restorations. The great monastery of Syon
was re-established, and the Priory of St.

John of Jerusalem. The Benedictines, under Abbot Feckenham, came back to Westminster in November ; the Carthusians, too, returned to Sheen, and there were hopes of restoring beautiful ruined Glastonbury to its Benedictine founders, but funds fell short.

The Legate succeeded Gardiner as Chancellor of Cambridge, and in October, 1556, he was elected to the same office at Oxford. There the shrine of St. Frideswide, patron of the university, had been grossly desecrated in the previous reign. The relics of the Saint, which had rested there for centuries, had been actually removed from her tomb in Christ Church to make room for the body of Peter Martyr's wife, an apostate nun, who had expressed a desire to be buried there. The Legate ordered the body of the unhappy woman to be removed, and the ashes of the Saint—which had been hidden in a corner of the church by a few pious Catholics—restored to their resting place. At Cambridge, a few months later, on the petition of the whole university, the bones of two notorious, persecuting heretics were removed from the churches in which they were buried, and interred in unconsecrated ground.

Pope Paul IV.

THE GREAT VICTORY

We touch now that period of Pole's life, when, but for his perfect humility and obedience, the sea of suffering into which he was plunged must have engulfed him. In order to grasp the circumstances we must glance for a moment at the reigning Pope, Paul IV., now eighty years old—a fiery Neapolitan whose ruling passion was hatred of the tyrant Spaniard, from whom his own beautiful country had suffered so greatly. His personally austere and blameless life and " great qualities were vitiated by a fierce and obstinate temper, a haughty and aspiring disposition, a mind incapable of yielding to opposition and greedy, above all things, of command," says a Catholic priest.* The great sovereigns who revered him as the Vicar of Christ and their spiritual lord, disliked and despised him as a temporal monarch—though it is perfectly clear, even from the unedifying records of the time, that the aged Pope was animated by but two ideas—the furtherance of God's Kingdom in the Catholic Church and the salvation of his country ; though his judgment was warped by his ungovernable temper.

* T. Phillips. " Life of Cardinal Pole," Vol. ii. p. 198.

Matters were terribly hard just now, from a political standpoint, for the Legate. England, of course, was definitely committed to Spain, and Spain was now openly in arms against the Holy Father, who was doing his best to expel Philip from his kingdom of Naples. At the same time England was in deadly hostility on her own account with France, and France was in close alliance with the Pope. Paul IV.'s "mad prank," as the Emperor contemptuously called it, was to fortify Rome, as he not unnaturally lived in constant expectation of a siege. In September, 1556, we have a most touching letter of Pole's to Cardinal Farnese, who had written to him in bitter anger about the cutting down by the Pope for this purpose of the magnificent trees in the Farnese gardens—a very human letter, in which he expresses his opinion that it had been done simply to hurt his feelings! Pole writes that he is *assai sensuale* as to trees and gardens, which he loves, to regret deeply these, which it seems to him, embellished not only the Farnese gardens but the whole of Rome. To think of it gave him more pain than he could have believed himself capable of feeling for such a loss. In conclusion he begs his friend to forgive Don Orsini, their executioner, who was only acting under Papal orders. In this same month of September he conducted Queen Mary through the grounds of Lambeth Palace. In January, 1557, a further complication was made by the open declaration of war between France and Spain, and shortly after this Philip returned from the continent in order to enlist England as the formal ally of the latter. The Cardinal-archbishop at once retired from court to his See of Canterbury, where he would fain have resided always, had the Queen, who desired his continual presence and counsel, permitted it. He could not, as Papal Legate, appear in public at the court of Paul IV.'s political enemy ; but he paid a private visit to Philip, where his extraordinary tact and delicacy stood him once more in good stead.

Whatever may he said against Philip, he at least treated England well ; and his character, in contemporary records, appears in such a light that one is inclined to feel that he has, on the whole, been rather maligned by history ! And then the blow fell—a thunderbolt from a cloudless sky. Paul IV., smarting with the mortification of failure, determined to recall all his legates from Spanish possessions, as countries rebellious to the Holy See. On May 15, 1557, he cancelled both Pole's commission as Legate *de latere*, and that of *Legatus natus*, which he held in right of his archbishopric of Canterbury. There was universal horror in England at this proceeding. Philip and Mary, who certainly had a claim to be heard, wrote strongly to the Pope, who replied on June 14, that though he could not revoke Pole's recall as Legate *de latere* he might still retain the title of *Legatus natus*. But he was still recalled.

Meanwhile the Cardinal, who had been deeply shocked at the whole proceeding, was so much missed at court that both King and Queen summoned him to take part in the council ; and on June 7, he had reluctantly given his consent to the war with France, during which England lost the very last of her French possessions—Calais.

The King and Queen again wrote to the Pope, pointing out the irremediable harm it would do the country, so lately returned from schism, if the Legate who had been the instrument of its restoration were recalled before his work of reform was finished. But Paul IV. had already made up his mind. On June 14, he proposed in consistory a new cardinal, Friar Peto, Queen Mary's confessor, a Minorite observant of Greenwich. He was a gentle and holy old man, of humble origin, now eighty years old, and totally unfitted for the position of Legate *de latere* in England, in which Paul IV. most illogically proposed to substitute him for Cardinal Pole.

To Mary, the Pope wrote that having once recalled the Cardinal he could not revoke his command; but that being quite as aware as she was of the necessity of a legate in England he had elevated Friar Peto to that dignity; and his cardinal's hat was even now on its way. This was in spite of the strongest warnings by Sir Edward Carne, English ambassador in Rome, who, to judge from his extraordinarily interesting despatches, seems to have spoken his mind with perfect frankness throughout the whole affair. At the same time the Pope sent an official recall to Pole, though his acceptance of the archbishopric of

Canterbury had been on the understanding that he should henceforth be allowed to reside there.

Mary was furious. She felt that England was being sacrificed to the Pope's obstinacy —not realising that God could work by Peto as He could by Pole. She sent messengers to Calais to have all despatches from the Pope stopped—including the new cardinal's hat, until she had obtained from Rome an answer to a further remonstrance. But fortunately for her, Pole discovered this, and also her temporary suppression of his recall. With all solemnity he assured her that the commands of no earthly monarch could come before the Pope; and he firmly refused the petition of Queen and council to continue his title and state as Legate *de latere*, both of which he immediately discarded. He then wrote a long letter of explanation to the Pope, and waited for his final decision.

Meanwhile, on July 2, the Pope, finding, it is to be feared, that it would be impossible to carry out the recall without some valid reason, had more than hinted to Sir Edward Carne that Pole's presence was required on a charge of heresy. It is only too evident that Paul IV.'s jealousy of Pole's Spanish influence, and his desire to withdraw him at all costs, led him to prefer a charge which he could not have seriously believed for an instant, but which Pole could not refuse to answer.

That the Angelical Cardinal, *carnifex et flagellum ecclesiæ Anglicanæ*, as he was described by his Protestant " successor " at Canterbury,* known throughout Christendom as a champion of the Faith, as well as for the purity of his spotless life, should be the victim of such an inexplicable charge can only be comprehended by considering those brought against his Master.

A month later, on August 7, Queen Mary's remonstrance reached Rome, and was presented by Sir Edward Carne. The Pope, who seemed at first inclined to treat the matter jestingly, having read it " stood a great while with a heavy countenance, saying nothing."† At last, telling Carne it was a weighty matter which needed deliberation, he dismissed him. One cannot but feel great pity for the aged Pope on

* Parker.
† " State Papers of Queen Mary." Foreign Series.
1557.

whose shoulders the burden of temporal power weighed so heavily.

Mary pointed out clearly that his action in recalling Pole was doing infinite harm among heretics, and even Catholics; amongst whom the incredible and infamous whisper of heresy was fast spreading, so that men were asking if the Cardinal-legate himself was suspected who then could be safe?

No one knew better than Paul IV. the futility of the charge, which was manufactured out of the old story of Pole's leniency to Lutherans; and of his inclining at the General Council, rather to the teaching of St. Basil and St. Chrysostom on the question of justification, than to that of St. Augustine, whose opinion was more generally received. Paul had himself twice publicly denounced these "charges," the second time when Pole became Archbishop; and Mary did not fail to remind him of this, saying that the heresy—if any—must have occurred within the last year when the Cardinal was exercising legatine duties! " His Holiness," says Carne on August 14, " is so wedded to his own opinion, and so terrible to such as speak against him that [the cardinals] hold their tongues, and let him do what he will." He was all this time cruelly harassed and grieved about the terrible Spanish war proceeding in Italy. However, a fortnight later the Pope discussed the Queen's letter in consistory, but it was an unfavourable moment. Those cardinals friendly to the Queen (says Carne), "perceiving his holiness to be in ... choler," moved that they should wait until the special messenger sent by Pole could be heard. This was his datary, Monsignor Ormaneto,* who was thereupon bidden to wait on the Pope without delay ; but though he did wait nearly twenty-four hours, the Pope refused him audience, merely accepting Pole's letter of explanation, which had been delayed seven weeks. " His Holiness," says Carne, " is in a peck of troubles, and his proceedings are such as satisfy no man."

However, on September 12, 1557, peace was concluded with Spain, largely by Mary's influence ; and Paul IV., overjoyed, promised to consider Pole's recall in consistory ; but, doubtless because he thought it best to let the matter drop, he did not do

* Bishop of Padua, 1570.

so. Nothing further was said about the recall, or the reasons for it, which the Pope, not unnaturally, seems to have wished to forget. Meantime, poor Friar Peto, whose election was most unpopular in England, was in an anomalous position which to his humble nature was intensely trying. He was looked upon as a sort of rival candidate to the beloved Cardinal, and mocked and insulted when he appeared in public. It is even said that his death, in April, 1558, was caused by a blow thus received. In any case he was the greatest sufferer, and an absolutely innocent one.

About the middle of December, 1557, Pole appealed to the Pope's nephew, Cardinal Caraffa, to beg the Holy Father to settle, once for all, the question of the still uncancelled recall, and the heresy charge. It was breaking his heart, but he does not say so. Referring to his old friendship for the Pope, and to the work in England, which is " not his, but God's," he says he cannot understand why " he should so strenuously impede me from serving God and His church, and seek to do me such great dishonour, as never cardinal nor legate, however worthlessly he might have

served, had ever received from any pontiff."
He dwelt on the fact that no charge of heresy
had been made against him at his formal
recall. Even this letter, if the Pope ever
saw it, made no impression ; though a few
months later (March 17, 1558) Carne gives
it as his opinion that "His Holiness is
somewhat acrazed." Possibly this is the
most charitable solution.

At the end of March Pole wrote a last
dignified letter of appeal and remonstrance,
and henceforth, as far as Paul IV. was
concerned, the matter completely dropped.

But Pole's gentle heart was broken. This
last suffering had been keen enough to com-
plete the martyrdom of the martyr's son.
His health, too, was failing, as was also the
Queen's. Writing to Philip on September
5, 1558, and again on the 26th, he tells him
he is suffering from a "double quartan
ague," which "at his age and with his
constitution" seriously indisposes him. He
knew that the end was near.

In his will, drawn up a little later, after
a touching allusion to the Pope, whose
blessing he asks, he leaves a number of
legacies—Priuli to be his heir, and co-
executor with certain ecclesiastics. We

have some deeply pathetic details from Monsignor Priuli on this matter.* A few days before the Cardinal's death, Geoffrey, the brother who had so deeply wronged his family, died, leaving numerous sons and daughters, and " a small property scarcely sufficing to maintain them in poverty." " And these " says his friend, " are the poor relations to whom his right reverend lordship desired that part of his property should be distributed. You must know that during his life time both in Italy and here, the Cardinal never failed to succour them, though he never asked or received anything . . . for them or for any one else, either friend, relation or dependent on him in any manner." No one will ever know all his beautiful, secret charity.

" My belief," says the compiler of the Venetian Calendar,† " is that he did more to maintain the repute of his country for high breeding, scholarship, integrity and consistency, than any other Englishman I ever heard of ; " and this seems to have been the universal contemporary opinion. All who knew him, loved him.

* " Venetian Calendar," vi. (iii.), 1287.
† *Ibid.* v., p. xi., *preface.*

Priuli, however, refused to accept anything from the Cardinal. His legacy, he said, was his friendship with Pole. But he asked for his friend's diurnal and breviary, which he used until his death, scarcely two years later.

At the end of September Pole heard of the death of the Emperor ; and on October 4, he sent his chaplain to the Queen, to lay before her an account of the temporal matters of his legateship and archbishopric, and then gave himself wholly to preparation for death. The common report of his vast wealth was dissipated when after his death Priuli met the Earl of Rutland on behalf of Elizabeth and proved, by the careful and minute accounts kept of the Legate's expenditure, that all his revenues from his own property abroad, as well as the little he had received for his expenses in England, had all been spent in providing for " the expense of many ministers," to whom he had to give " board and stipend." Of the ecclesiastical property ceded by the Queen and placed unreservedly in his hands, the accurate accounts kept by Henry Pening showed that under the management of several bishops, every crown had been disbursed for the church. In order to obtain enough money for the funeral it was even considered necessary to sell his plate, nearly all of which he had brought with him from the continent—some of which he had doubtless used in his early days at Padua.

Queen Mary, too, was dying, and daily messages passed between the cousins.* Daily was the Holy Sacrifice offered in the chamber of the dying Cardinal, and daily, weak as he was from fever, he would be lifted from his bed to fall on his knees at the elevation. He communicated daily, and seemed to live in the visible presence of God. Priuli writes : † " When from the progress of the disease his lordship was obliged to keep constantly in bed, yet wishing to communicate as he had already done frequently, he chose to hear Mass, and get out of bed at that part where he had to communicate although unable without very great inconvenience and fatigue ; and when about to communicate, being supported by two persons (as otherwise he could not have kept his feet) he bowed his head almost to the

* The Queen at St. James's Palace, the Cardinal at Lambeth.
† " Venetian Calendar," vi. (iii.), 1292.

ground, and with many tears and sobs said inwardly the *Confiteor*. When I saw him thus I thought I saw the picture of our Lord's Blessed Mother as she is represented at the foot of the cross, supported by the two Maries ; and in truth I never witnessed in any other person such deep expression of contrition and devotion, so true and cordial. He communicated several times even after this, and till the last day chose to hear daily not only the Mass, but also the office, and three hours before his death he heard vespers and compline."

On November 15, both the Queen and Cardinal received extreme unction; "after which," says Priuli, "it seemed as if they rallied, and were much comforted, according to the fruit of that most holy medicine . . . and gave clear proof of increasing spiritual vigour, not less than corporal improvement." Nevertheless on this day the hopeless condition of the Queen was gently broken to him.

Next day he heard Mass of the most Blessed Trinity, and communicated devoutly, sending and receiving thereafter affectionate messages from Queen Mary. He was growing rapidly weaker, burnt with the paroxysms of the intermittent fever. On November 17, the Feast of St. Hugh of Lincoln, came the end. " On the next morning [*i.e.*, the 17th] which was his last," writes his faithful friend, " he listened to the Mass of the Angel, who, we may verily believe, accompanied that sainted soul to Heaven." One of his Italian attendants broke to him, sooner than was intended, the news of the death of the Queen while hearing Mass of St. Hugh ; when she " yielded her mylde and glorious spirit into ye Hande of her Maker ;* at the very moment of the " levacion of the Sacrament."

He received the news in silence, remaining some time in prayer ; after which he spoke to Priuli, and the Bishop of St. Asaph of the wonderful way in which God's providence had dealt with both Mary and himself, who were near relations, and had so much in common—how both had suffered and laboured for the same cause, and were now dying together. He could not but fear for the troubles coming upon the country (for he was not unacquainted with its future Queen), " yet by God's grace, that same faith and reliance on the Divine

* Cotton MSS.

Providence which had ever comforted him in all his adversities greatly consoled him likewise in this so grievous a final catastrophe."

Then, for in spite of his serenity "the blow had entered into his flesh," he felt that the end was close. Another cruel paroxysm of fever left him with "more intense cold than he had hitherto experienced." He asked that the Book of Prayers for the dying should be placed at hand. "Now is the time to use it," he said gently, when the bishop showed it to him.

"He then," says his devoted friend, "had vespers repeated as usual, and the compline, which part of the office then remained for him to hear; and this was about two hours before sunset." "*In manus tuas, Domine, commendo spiritum meum*" were probably the last words he heard, on earth. "In fine it was evident that as in health that sainted soul was ever turned to God, so likewise in this long and troublesome infirmity did it continue thus, until his end, which he made so placidly that he seemed to sleep rather than die."

His body lay in state in Lambeth Palace,

where four masses were daily said for the repose of his gentle soul; and then, by his own wish, taken to his Cathedral at Canterbury, "in a sumptuous herse," in solemn procession, being met there by a "great concourse of clergy and people."

Here in the chapel of St. Thomas of Canterbury the body of the last of his successors was laid to rest; with the simple inscription: "*Beati mortui qui in Domino moriuntur,*" over the words "*Depositum Cardinalis Poli.*"

* * * *

Beati pacifici . . . beati mundi corde, quoniam ipsi Deum videbunt.

APPENDIX

AN ACT OF THANKSGIVING FOR THE RECONCILIATION OF ENGLAND

THE following remarkable prayers were found by the Editor written in the end of a magnificent copy of Pynson's edition of the Sarum Missal (1520) which is preserved among the treasures of the famous Pepysian Library at Magdalene College, Cambridge.

As far as is known, no other copy of these prayers is in existence, and they have never before been printed. They consist, evidently, of what is known as an *Oratio imperata* with corresponding Secret and Post communion, *i.e.*, special prayers ordered by authority to be said at Mass after the collects for the day on some particular occasion or for some special intention.

These prayers are headed :

Orationes dicende in missis pro agendis deo gratiis de reconciliatione regni cum

225   P

ecclesia catholica : that is to say, " Prayers to be said at Mass, to give God thanks for the reconciliation of the kingdom with the Catholic Church." They were, no doubt, ordered by Cardinal Pole, under whose direction they will have been composed (if he did not himself write them) to be said or sung in solemn thanksgiving for the Reconciliation of England on that great St. Andrew's Day, 1554. Probably they were to be used every year on the anniversary of that glorious event. They have thus an enormous and most pathetic interest for English Catholics. They inevitably suggest a comparison with those that Cardinal Vaughan ordered to be recited year by year in the Mass of the English Martyrs, in memory of the Consecration of England to Our Lady and St. Peter.

It will be interesting if it is possible to discover any allusion to these prayers in Pole's correspondence, and still more so if the order for their recital can be discovered among his papers.

D. B. C.

APPENDIX

ORATIO

Deus qui hoc regnum a catholice ecclesie unitate, et obedientia, satane malicia alienatum, ad eandem sub philippo et maria regibus, per romani pontificis, et sedis apostolice legatum, totius regni consensu, singulari tue benignitatis previlegio revocasti, concede quesumus, ut tanti beneficii semper memores, in vere religionis cultu, et catholice ecclesie unitate atque obedientia te protegente constanter perseveremus, utque reliqui populi qui ab ea recesserunt ad eandem nostro exemplo revertantur : per dominum, &c.

Deus a quo salvator noster Jesus christus ne fides petri deficere[t] orans, pro sua reverentia est exauditus, concede precamur omnibus nobis a sismate et erroribus quibus immersi fuimus, tua clementia mirabiliter liberatis, eam in fide constantiam que ab apostolica sede nunquam nos liberare* (sic) sinat : per eundem dominum, &c.

Presta quesumus omnipotens deus, ut nos qui per immensam misericordiam tuam ad catholice ecclesie unitatem, et vicarii uni-

* This is apparently a corrupt reading for *aberrare*.

227

*geniti filii obedientiam a qua satane fraude
delusi longe recesseramus, tanquam oves
errantes reducti sumus, ita per gratiam tuam
in vere obedientie fructibus crescamus, ut
nostro exemplo et qui in ea manent confirmentur,
et rebelles te inspirante ad eandem revocentur :
per eundem dominum, &c.*

We append a translation which we have
made as literal as possible.

PRAYER.

O God, Who by the singular privilege of
Thy kindness, hast, with the consent of the
whole realm, through the legate of the
Roman Pontiff and the Apostolic See, recalled this kingdom, alienated by Satan's
malice from the unity and obedience of the
Catholic Church, back to the same under
Kings Philip and Mary : grant we beseech
Thee, that always being mindful of so great
a benefit, we may constantly persevere,
under Thy protection, in the worship of the
true religion and in the unity and obedience
of the Catholic Church, that the other
peoples which have gone astray may, by
our example, return to it once more :
Through our Lord, &c.

APPENDIX

SECRET.

O God, by Whom our Saviour Jesus Christ, praying that the faith of Peter might not fail, was heard for His reverence; grant, we beseech Thee, to all of us, who by Thy clemency have been wonderfully delivered from the schism and errors in which we were immersed, that constancy in the faith which may never permit us to stray from the Apostolic See; Through the same, &c.

POST COMMUNION.

Grant, we beseech Thee, Almighty God, that we who by Thy immense mercy have been brought back like erring sheep to the unity of the Catholic Church and to the obedience of the Vicar of Thine only-begotten Son, from which deluded by the craft of Satan we had gone far astray, may so by Thy grace increase in the fruits of true obedience, that by our example both those who remain in it may be confirmed and the rebellious may be inspired by Thee to return to the same; Through the same, &c.